CONFIDENCE FOR

LIVING
WEALTHY

UNLOCKING GOD'S UNLIMITED
RESOURCES FOR YOUR LIFE

KEITH JOHNSON

Confidence for Living Wealthy: Unlocking God's Unlimited Resources for Your Life

KJI Publishing

PO Box 15001

Spring Hill, Florida 34604

(352) 597-8775

Cover design by: Martijn van Tilborgh

ISBN Trade Paper: 978-0-9855167-2-7

ISBN EBook: 978-0-9855167-5-8

For Worldwide Distribution, Printed in the U.S.A.

1 2 3 4 5 6 / 21 20 19 18

CONTENTS

OTHER BOOKS BY DR. KEITH JOHNSON

DEDICATION

I dedicate this book to my conditioning coach Micheal Maysonet. Without your wisdom, intuition, and care for me at the gym on December 7, 2016, when I had my heart attack, I would not be alive today to write this book. Thanks for caring about my well-being, insisting that I go to the emergency room, and being with me until you were sure I was okay. Your dedication to serving others has made you a very wealthy man.

ACKNOWLEDGMENTS

FIRST OF ALL, A SPECIAL BIG THANK YOU to Jerret Hammond. Your dedication to helping me write and brand this book has been a fresh wind in my sail. Thanks for being there for me during the most challenging year of my life.

A special thank you to Dr. Larry Keefauver, my friend and book writing coach, for helping me outline the thoughts in this book.

Thank you to Martijn van Tilborgh for your marketing expertise and the original idea for the cover design. Thank you for pushing me out of my normal branding box.

Thank you to Angela R. Shears for your editing work and expertise in taking my words and making them come alive.

And I especially thank my wife, Dr. Bonnie Johnson. This book is the story of our journey together to Living Wealthy as we have stood on Proverbs 3:5-6. You have supported me in some of my darkest moments. Thank you for always being the sunshine on my path to greatness.

WEALTH.

The very word invokes images, feelings, opinions, facts and figures—and memories.

But what has God always intended wealth to be?

The answer is found within.

CHAPTER 1

MORE THAN I EVER THOUGHT POSSIBLE

WELCOME TO *CONFIDENCE FOR LIVING WEALTHY!* Living Wealthy is all about your magnificent future. It's about living life at the highest level of your true potential. It's all about creating a holistic lifestyle of *spiritual, mental, physical, relational, professional,* and *financial success.*

The book title implies that this is another "prosperity book." But no. Living Wealthy isn't just about money, career success, bigger houses, and fancy cars. It's more about you becoming the person you were designed to be so you can achieve your God-given destiny.

On December 7, 2016, I was in the best shape physically in my entire life, with only 13 percent body fat. I went to the gym for a workout with my trainer when BAM! It suddenly hit me. A full-blown heart attack. Doctors refer to it as the "widow maker" because most people die almost instantly.

I actually drove myself to the hospital, and 3 hours later was informed that they had saved my life. I thanked God. The cardiologist was scheduled to examine my heart the next day to see what caused the problem.

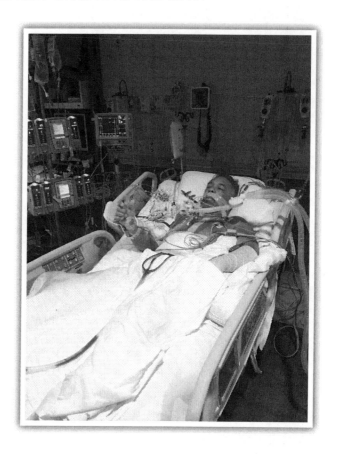

As I lay on the table, watching my heart beat on the monitor beside my bed, the cardiologist informed me that I needed quintuple bypass surgery to correct the blocked arteries. A short time later I was told this was one of the most dangerous surgeries—with a possibility that I would not survive.

I spent the next two days being prepared for surgery. It was the longest two days of my life. Lying in the bed, I reflected on what I had heard the late Dr. Myles Monroe say frequently at several conferences I was part of:

Where are the most expensive pieces of real estate in the world? Is it the diamond mines of South Africa? Oceanfront property in Hawaii? Or the oil fields of Saudi Arabia? I think the most expensive pieces of real estate are the graveyards around the world. Why? Because they are full of people who went to the grave without fulfilling their potential. The grave is full of books that should have been written. Songs that were never heard. Businesses that were never started and cures of diseases that have never been discovered.

I couldn't shift my mind away from these thoughts, *What if I had died yesterday? What if I die tomorrow in surgery? Would I die with regrets that I didn't fulfill everything God wanted me to do while on this earth, or would I go to the grave fulfilled that I had finished my race?*

FAILURES

My mind instantly went back to my past and where I came from. Life had always seemed a struggle for me. Nothing came easily. I certainly wasn't voted "Most Likely to Succeed."

For instance:

- I flunked kindergarten, and my teacher told me I was a "slow learner." For years I believed she meant I was stupid.

- When I turned 7 years of age, my parents divorced. I blamed myself and thought it was because I was a bad boy.

- By the time I was in fifth grade, I could barely read and write, and almost failed that year.

- When I was 8, my mother married an alcoholic who verbally and psychologically abused our family, including me.

- My biological father joined a motorcycle gang called Satan's Escorts and was a drug addict and alcoholic.

- At 10 years of age, I was hit by a motorcycle while riding my bicycle; my leg was broken so badly that the doctors said I would never walk without a limp.

- When I was 14, I smoked my first marijuana joint—with my father. And when I was 16, he taught me how to sell drugs for a living.

- By the time I was 22, I was still not a good reader and had never read an entire book.

- I was so insecure at 23 that I was afraid to call the phone company for overcharging me $250.

ACHIEVEMENTS

Then, as I lay in the hospital bed, alone with my thoughts, my mind leapt to what I had achieved up to that point in my life:

- How I traveled internationally over the past 5 years to seventeen-plus nations to speak in megachurches.

- How I had just completed a one-year tour speaking to more than 100,000 business leaders for a seminar company about which Fox News reported, "This conference is where the most successful and inspirational people in the country share their secrets with you."

- I was even featured in *Woman's World* magazine, which graciously called me America's Ultimate Coach, which still makes me smile to this day.

- My confidence-boosting message landed me in featured segments on Fox News, ABC News, CBS News, TBN, Daystar, and other major broadcasts worldwide.

- Although I could barely read, my book was released by the second largest publisher in the world—and quickly became an Amazon best seller.

- Soon after, I purchased and moved into the house of my dreams. I filled my garages with the cars of my dreams as well.

- I even became completely debt free without going bankrupt (even though I had over $180,000 in credit card debt).

Some believe that people on their deathbed aren't thinking about money. Well, let me tell you, I definitely was thinking about it. I wanted to make sure my wife knew about our finances, and I gave her information she needed to know if something happened to me. I was proud of myself for saving enough money so my wife wouldn't have any financial pressures if the surgery wasn't successful.

As I looked back over my entire life, I remembered the day when I was 23 years old and I had to search through every drawer in my trailer to gather enough pennies so I could run to Taco Bell and buy two 39-cent tacos for dinner.

And then I thought about how I had been radically blessed by God to live a lifestyle only the top 2 percent of people in the entire world ever get to experience. Reflecting on how I had maximized my potential for the past 25 years, I concluded that if I had died the day before or if I were to die tomorrow, I would die with no regrets.

LIVING WEALTHY MINDSET

YOUR GOD-GIVEN ASSIGNMENT, LEFT UNDONE, TURNS INTO REGRET.

I define *true wealth* as *maximizing your potential.* This book is all about giving you CONFIDENCE for LIVING WEALTHY so you can die completely emptied and fulfilled.

ONE MORE MESSAGE

After I survived open-heart surgery, God told me He wasn't through with me—I had one more message to deliver to the world. He said:

> My leaders and people are struggling to get the resources they need to fulfill their destiny. They are feeling the hurtful sting of their own unleashed potential and lack of financial understanding. The power of confidence and the holistic principles of wealth I have taught you will bring healing and hope to the masses.

I must admit. For years I have resisted teaching on wealth, money, or finances because I feared being labeled a "prosperity preacher." However, after hearing from God, with renewed confidence and courage, I have decided to take any negative punches from "religious" people in order to focus my energies on bringing healing to those who need it. In the end, I know it will be worth it to hear my Father say, "Well done, My son!" So while I am here on earth, I will be obedient to share that message, and in turn witness millions of people's lives being changed.

When you change the way you look at something, what you look at will change.
–Wayne Dyer
Best-Selling Author of *Excuses Begone!*

WHAT I LEARNED FROM A DEAD LOBSTER

Three short months after my open-heart surgery, I was back on the road speaking again. Prior to my visit to the state of Maine, I thought I had experienced everything life had to offer. However, after I completed my seminar, my host took me to an exquisite restaurant to eat fresh Maine lobster.

Ohmygosh! I thought I had died and gone to heaven! I had never seen a lobster that big nor had I tasted anything as succulent and delicious. I looked at my host and said, "I think God kept me alive just to experience eating fresh Maine lobster." We both laughed and continued to eat. Later that night while in my hotel room, I heard, "Keith, when you were in the hospital, you thought you had experienced it all. But I want you to know that I have places, people, experiences, blessings, and financial rewards waiting for you in your future BEYOND what you have currently experienced. Just as you are blown away by what I have done in your life so far, rest assured that what is coming is even better, brighter, and bigger."

DISPELLING THE LIE!

You may have bought into the big lie that "This is the best my life, church, ministry, or business can get." You're wrong! You have only experienced life at your current level. King Solomon reminds us,

"The end of a thing is better than its beginning" (Ecclesiastes 7:8).

You will learn in the following pages how to break through your current limitations and experience life at levels that "eye has not seen nor ears have heard." Are you ready to take your first step?

THE FIRST STEP TO LIVING WEALTHY: SHRINK YOUR EGO!

I will never forget the day that I went to a wealth-building seminar and the speaker punched me in the face with the truth of my current situation. She put me on a new path to changing my life.

This is how the speaker opened the seminar with her transformational message:

I have seven questions to ask you:

1. Stand if you have credit card debt (95% of the crowd stood).
2. Stand if you only have one source of income (3% more of thecrowd stood).
3. Stand if you don't have 6 months' worth of money in the bank for an emergency fund (the last 2% of the crowd stood).

Wow! Everyone was standing and she still had four more questions to ask us. Then with absolute confidence, she said:

At this point in your life you have no legitimate right to have an opinion about the subject of wealth, money, or prosperity!

Why? Because you don't know anything about it!

Why? Because you don't have any of it!

Why? Because you mismanaged it!

Why? Because nobody has ever taught you how to think and behave wealthy!

So you've spent the majority of your life playing follow the follower. You watched the followers...listened to the followers... were influenced by the followers...agreed with followers...started thinking and behaving like the followers, and now you have created a lifestyle just like the masses of the blind leading the blind. You're spending sleepless nights worrying about financial issues, afraid of what your future is going to look like.

I have to admit. At first, I was offended and wanted to walk out of the seminar. My big fat ego screamed, "Who does this lady think she is? I have studied the biblical principles of stewardship for years."

Then I heard another quiet voice, "Yes, but she is right. You're in debt up to your eyeballs, you're living paycheck to paycheck, you owe more money for your car than it's worth, you have no real significant money in the bank, and you and your wife are stressed and continue to get in fights over your money issues."

Before real change started to happen in my life, I had to shrink my ego. Yes. I had a big ego with a tiny bank account. I quickly started to learn that a small ego has the possibility, with the right strategy, to produce a BIG bank account.

LIVING WEALTHY MINDSET

SHRINKING YOUR EGO CAUSES YOU TO LEARN MORE. WHEN YOU **LEARN** MORE, YOU WILL NATURALLY **EARN** MORE. NOT JUST MONEY BUT ALSO INFLUENCE, IMPACT, AND RESPECT.

In my youth, I thought I knew everything. The older I get and the more I learn, the more I realize how little I know. I need to continue to learn and grow. Especially if I'm experiencing negative results in certain areas of my life.

The hardcore truth will always offend your ego and mind when you first hear it. The Holy Spirit has to offend your mind because life change starts with brand-new thoughts and ideas.

Stick with me throughout this book as we embark on my personal transformational journey of losing everything with only a dream and a laptop to becoming an internationally acclaimed confidence coach and speaker.

UNLEARN AND RELEARN

Let's start by praying what I call my potential prayer: "Lord, shrink my ego so I can learn more!"

We will do two important things together:

1. *Unlearn* errors taught in the past.
2. *Relearn* what we need to know for the future.

Yes, there is work to be done! But there is a succulent, fresh lobster dinner waiting for you at the end. Trust me, it will be worth all the hard work to read and learn from this book—cover to cover.

ARE YOU READY FOR POSITIVE LIFE CHANGES?

Here's what I know! Life change is possible. You're not stuck where you are. Confidence is the power you need to overcome the fear that will surface when you start really reaching for *Living Wealthy*.

You may be:

- Afraid that people won't like you if you become wealthy.
- Afraid you will turn away from your walk with God.
- Afraid of people criticizing you and rejecting you.
- Afraid that wealth may change your personality.
- Afraid that if you try to become wealthy, you may fail.

Fear conjures up all kinds of tragic imaginations concerning your future. *Confidence* offers your imagination all kinds of achievement, happiness, success, wealth, abundance, and miracles.

LIVING WEALTHY MINDSET

CONFIDENCE IS AN EXPECTATION THAT YOUR FUTURE IS GOING TO BE BRIGHTER, BETTER, AND BIGGER THAN YOUR PRESENT.

Fear of the future causes you to hold on tightly to the secure known of the present, while *confidence in the future* empowers you with a spirit of innovation to change. When you start fearing the future, you typically stop moving forward, and progress comes to a screeching halt.

It's essential that you have confidence for the future. Because without confidence, you can't have the faith necessary to move forward and change.

21

My new friend, before we get started, I want you to think about this: What if everything you have ever learned about:

- Wealth
- God and money
- Work
- The rich
- The middle class
- The poor

...is 100 percent wrong?

You need *confidence* to actually doubt everything you have been taught. But think about this, if what you have learned isn't working for you and possibly those you lead, either God is a liar or we have been taught to think and behave wrongly.

I choose to believe that God doesn't lie. I choose to believe that if I'm not getting results in my life, then I must change my belief systems so I can live the life God expects of me, *the abundant life.*

To have confidence for Living Wealthy, you need to be a contrarian, a bold risk-taker, an outsider. You will face challenges by living life outside the masses' group-think mentality, but you will also reap all the wonderful rewards that the "normal thinking" people will never generate.

You must be willing to walk away from everything you have believed in the past in order to walk into God's divine destiny for your life in the future. If you're ready to forget everything you've been taught about wealth, ready to walk into a greater reality of what God has for you—then suspend disbelief and let's run together toward *Confidence for Wealthy Living.*

• • •

Before we start, it's time to make a choice. Which one of these do you want for your future?

☐ Living Wealthy
☐ Living Average
☐ Living Poor
☐ None of Above

[Check One]

I knew you would pick the right one—let's go!

CHAPTER 2

DEFINING THE POTENTIAL OF LIVING WEALTHY

WHAT HAS TO STOP AND WHAT HAS TO START IN ORDER TO SUCCEED?

Do you feel as if God wants you to make a huge difference in the world, yet you feel stuck where you are with limited support, time, and resources? Have you ever thought to yourself, *I should be a lot further along in life than I am right now?*

That thought came to me March 16, 2002. That was the day I experienced mental, emotional, spiritual, and total financial destruction. I knew in my core that God called me to more. I had dreams of traveling to different countries of the world and speaking and inspiring thousands of people to achieve their destiny and purpose in life.

I wanted to be an inspiration to those in poverty, to help provide a ladder of strategies so they could move from where they were to where they really wanted to be. I wanted to share what I discovered to major television and radio show audiences.

I had dreams of publishing best-selling books, even books for children. I wanted to educate thousands of people to be world-class leaders and become the best at what they do. But nothing, and I mean nothing, at that moment was happening—at least that's what I thought.

LIVING WEALTHY MINDSET

WHEN IT SEEMS AS IF NOTHING IS HAPPENING, DURING THOSE QUIET, INVISIBLE, AND DARK TIMES INSIDE YOU, BELOW THE SURFACE—KNOW THAT GOD IS PREPARING YOU FOR A BIGGER AND BETTER FUTURE.

When I started taking steps toward fulfilling my destiny, I saw glimpses of my dream coming true as I traveled and spoke to groups in a variety of small, local churches across the United States. I published my first book, and was invited to speak on local television programs.

Trying to get from where I was to where I wanted to go felt like pushing a huge boulder up Mount Everest. I was working harder than ever, but gaining no traction. This was a frustrating season in my life. Why? I had been awakened to my God-given potential—and I wanted to achieve the goals set before me as soon as possible.

LIVING WEALTHY MINDSET

POTENTIAL IS SIMPLY THE GAP BETWEEN WHERE YOU ARE AND WHERE YOU COULD BE.

What is and what isn't "potential"?

- Potential isn't the person you are right now; it unleashes the person you can grow to become.

- Potential isn't what you're doing right now; it empowers what you can do in your future.

- Potential isn't what you have right now (your home, car, or the size of your bank account); potential is taking advantage of your strengths to increase your finances, buy a better car, and live in a comfortable home.

- Potential isn't how many people you are helping and serving right now; potential is realizing the multitudes more you can help and serve tomorrow.

LIVING WEALTHY MINDSET

THERE IS NO ACHE IN THE HUMAN HEART LIKE UNREALIZED POTENTIAL.

When there's a "potential" gap between where you are and where you want to be, you will feel pain, frustration, and discontent. Your mind may be telling you right now, *I'm not in pain. I have everything I need.* I know those thoughts. That was what I thought because at the time my ego, combined with self-doubt, was talking. *I'm doing okay, there's no need to upset the status quo. Sure there are things I'd like to have and do, but I'm better off than many other people.*

In the next few paragraphs, I will show you how a newly discovered life-changing truth positively shifted my life.

UNLEASHED POTENTIAL AND ADDICTION

The pain of my unleashed potential caused me to reach toward medication to bring temporary relief to my heart. The world is full of drugs that seduce you into thinking, in your moment of pain, that they can help you. Yet most only produce a temporary false feeling of pleasure—and a long-term sense of dependency on a deadly poison.

The elements of addiction are found in human nature, and the desire within all of us to make it through life with the least amount of pain and the highest amount of pleasure possible.
–Dr. Ted Roberts

Medication moves us from momentary pain to momentary pleasure. Different people settle on different types of medication that they think will solve the problem, any problem. Some medicate themselves with drugs, alcohol, sex, or even seemingly innocent vices like overeating, spending hours and hours in front of the television, gambling, or out-of-control shopping.

My healing medication came in the mail one sunny afternoon. I was shocked. I didn't even order it. I thought, *Now, this is just what I've been waiting for!* It was a prescription sent to me from Dr. American Express. This medication gave me temporary relief from the pain of my unfulfilled potential by enabling me to go to the mall and buy myself a new watch and clothes, and eat at a swanky new restaurant. That spending spree made me feel great—for the moment.

LIVING WEALTHY MINDSET

CREDIT CARDS GIVE THE INSTANT ILLUSION THAT YOU'RE RICH, BUT A BOUT WITH BAD DEBT BRINGS A LIFE CYCLE OF LACK. CONSUMER DEBT STRIPS YOUR FUTURE TO ENHANCE YOUR PRESENT—BUT EVENTUALLY STEALS YOUR CONFIDENCE.

When the pain resurfaced, I made another trip to the mall. It sure felt good to walk out carrying a new bag of clothes. Other times when I felt the pain of stagnation, a mouth-watering, garlic-buttered filet mignon and lobster tail at Capital Grille gave me relief—for the moment. Later every month, however, I felt the real pain of receiving the AmEx bill in the mail and realizing just how much my medication cost.

But, I was addicted and kept refilling my American Express prescription right up until I was notified that access to my card was cut off. And rightfully so. It wasn't unlike the bartender who cuts off a drunk who is out of control. Yet, I was outraged! How could they do this to me?!

After a week of not being able to use my credit card, I was elated when I received more medication in the mail! (Apparently, Dr. Visa was sympathetic to my plight.)

When I couldn't pay what I owed to American Express, I got cash advances from Visa to cover the payment. Soon, even my new drug dealer at Visa cut me off. Then one card after another started to pour in like shipments of cocaine from Colombia. I ended up with a total of 32 credit cards and more than $180,000 in debt.

This medication wasn't "God providing a way out," but rather a wolf in sheep's clothing. My financial situation was fragile. I realized that one tiny misstep and the whole house of cards would come tumbling down.

September 11, 2001. One of the most catastrophic crises to ever hit the United States. A small group of terrorists attacked the US by hijacking airplanes and crashing them into the World Trade Center towers and the Pentagon. Fear spread throughout the nation like a pandemic. People were too afraid to travel.

For a year, life seemed to come to a standstill—and my speaking business suddenly came to a screeching halt. No bookings, nowhere to speak, and ultimately no money coming in. For months I looked at a stack of bills on my desk with no clue how to pay them.

All of my credit cards were maxed out, and nobody would give me any more of my precious medication. Because of my bad judgment, I was placed on a "watch list" as "someone close to bankruptcy"—like some sort of terrorist inside the credit card reporting system.

LIVING WEALTHY MINDSET

NOTHING HUMBLES LIKE FAILURE. IT'S FAR BETTER TO HUMBLE YOURSELF NOW THAN TO BE HUMILIATED LATER.

Drowning in debt up to my eyeballs, without work, and absolutely no money in the bank, my wife and I sold everything we owned and moved in to my mother-in-law's spare bedroom. I jokingly say at many of my seminars, "Life can't get any worse than living with your mother-in-law. It was a living hell on earth!"

The truth is, that was the toughest year of my life, yet it was the greatest year of my life. It was a year that I would never trade or take away. I learned so much from that season. I learned that my heart was right, but my head had a lot of wrong in it.

So there I am on that fateful March 16 morning. My wife and mother-in-law went to get groceries. Sitting all alone at the breakfast nook, feeling sorry for myself, I cried out to God, "Lord, what am I missing? Why am I stuck here? I feel called to do the work You gave me, but I keep coming up short."

LIVING WEALTHY MINDSET

YOU CAN HAVE A GREAT HEART BUT AN EMPTY HEAD. PAIN IS A SIGN YOU NEED TO OPEN YOUR HEART AND HEAD FOR LEARNING.

God responded to me that day in a mighty way that set me on a trajectory that has not only changed my life, but also the lives of one million believers, achievers, and leaders as well. God simply said to me, "Keith, you lack confidence." That simple statement sent me on a 15-year quest to conquer my fears, uncertainties, and doubts. Today, I'm known worldwide as America's #1 Confidence Coach—because *potential* was the bridge between my past and current situation to an amazing future!

The gap between where you are now and where you could be is potential. The good news for you is that you can close that gap—with confidence. Understand this: *the attitude of confidence determines the altitude of success and wealth.* That's why the title of this book is *Confidence for Living Wealthy.*

LIVING WEALTHY MINDSET

THE GREATEST MISTAKE I MADE WAS **UNDERESTIMATING MY POTENTIAL.**

Wealth, as defined in this book, is simply maximizing your potential in every area of your life. Imagine with me for just a moment what your life would look like if you were firing on all cylinders:

- What levels of success could you achieve?
- What size impact could your ministry have?
- What size could your business become?

- What amount could you have in the bank?

Another question is not *if* you can leave your children an inheritance, but how many generations deep! Just imagine it. Visualize it.

It's time to leave the cult of mediocrity and wake up to your wealth potential!

More than 70 years ago, psychologist William James declared a major wake-up call about the temptation to become mediocre and average when he said:

Compared to what we ought to be, we are only half awake. Our fires are dampened, our drafts are checked, we are making use of only a small part of our mental and physical resources.

I've designed this book to give you the combination to unlock the unlimited resources that God has *already given you* to maximize your potential in every area of your life. We are going to take this concept further a little later in this book, so I encourage you to keep reading.

INVESTING IN YOURSELF

Only 10 percent of books purchased by adults are ever read all the way through. Don't rob yourself of all that God has for you. You invested in this book—now invest in yourself and read this thing cover to cover.

LIVING WEALTHY MINDSET

ADOPT THE BELIEF THAT YOUR OBSTACLES AND SETBACKS ARE OPPORTUNITIES TO INCREASE YOUR POTENTIAL.

Over the next 12 months, my life began to tell a different story. I majorly changed my way of thinking and working. I moved out from under my own stupidity and self-deception and admitted I was doing too much credit card spending and my addiction had caused me so much stress and robbed me from unleashing my full potential.

I made a commitment to study everything I could about unleashing human potential. I was tired of the pain in my life, and wanted to find real solutions to healing the pain of unleashed potential in millions of other people's lives as well.

When I made the choice to work on maximizing my full potential, my entire life started to quickly change for the better. My personal achievements, happiness, and income quickly increased. Today, I travel the world speaking at some of the largest churches and business conferences in the world. I live in the house of my dreams, drive the car of my dreams, and am totally debt-free, including credit cards.

I spend my time influencing the influencers of society, having coached senior pastors from small, medium, to mega-size churches; celebrities; government officials; business leaders; millionaires; and even a billionaire.

Dr. Abraham Maslow wrote, "One can choose to go back toward safety or forward toward growth. Growth must be chosen again and again; fear must be overcome again and again."

Just imagine what God could accomplish through you if you committed today to push past your fears and step onto the bridge of confidence leading to a lifetime of wealth.

Coaching Mantra:

- Your POTENTIAL is greater than your past.
- Your POTENTIAL is greater than your pain.
- Your POTENTIAL is greater than your opposition.
- Your POTENTIAL is greater than your lack.
- Your POTENTIAL is greater than your paycheck.

CHAPTER 3

MAXIMIZING THE SIX CONFIDENCE COMBINATIONS

UNLOCKING AND ACCESSING YOUR WEALTH-INTELLIGENCE POTENTIAL

WHAT CAUSES SOME PEOPLE to rise above the mediocre crowd and become more, do more, have more, and help many more people, while the majority tend to live meager lives, only helping a few people during their lifetime?

Human potential experts have been trying to answer this question for decades. In my season of pain, I started to study this subject for myself. I came across something interesting. In 1905, French psychologist Alfred Binet developed the first Intelligence Quotient (IQ) test. The thesis was that a high score on this test measured a person's intelligence, and ultimately could determine how much success the person would achieve in life.

After years of studying the IQs of individuals and their achievements, scientists learned a higher IQ doesn't necessarily have a direct correlation to a person's level of success. I'm sure you've seen this in your own life. All of us have brilliant family members or friends living far below their true potential. It's heartbreaking, isn't it?

LIVING WEALTHY MINDSET

INTELLIGENCE DOESN'T NECESSARILY EQUAL SUCCESS. THERE ARE MANY POOR COLLEGE PROFESSORS, AND MANY MILLIONAIRE HIGH SCHOOL DROPOUTS.

Another scientist suggested that the key ingredient to measuring human potential is Emotional Intelligence (EQ). This theory is based on the psychological understanding that thoughts produce emotions, emotions produce behavior, and behavior produces results. So if you can control your thoughts, you can control your emotions, you can control your behavior, and ultimately your results in life.

One author released a book suggesting that our Spiritual Quotient (SQ) is the key ingredient to maximizing our human potential. After crisscrossing the globe many times and speaking to many different church groups, I have observed that some of the most spiritual people I run into tend to be underachievers—including many ministers.

LIVING WEALTHY MINDSET

TO UNLEASH YOUR FULL POTENTIAL, YOU MUST KNOW BOTH THE PERSON AND THE PRINCIPLES OF JESUS.

For years I spent time developing a relationship with the *person* of Jesus, which produces peace in my life. However, I was ignorant about many of the *principles* of Jesus that would eventually produce prosperity for me. This, to me, is truly possessing a high SQ.

In my *LQ Solution* book, I wrote that all three of these ingredients: IQ, EQ, and SQ are important contributors toward unleashing potential.

However, your Leadership Quotient (LQ) is really the key ingredient to maximize human potential. Leadership Quotient is a composite measure of a person's leadership skills that positively influences people to join that leader in achieving desired outcomes that benefit others.

No matter how smart, how spiritually fit, or how emotionally stable you are, if you can't get people on your team to help you achieve your dream, your potential will always be limited. Why? Because one is too small a number for greatness. *It's teamwork that makes the dream work.* If you haven't read my *LQ Solution* book, I highly recommend grabbing it soon at www.LQSolution.com. It is filled with practical, proven-successful wisdom regarding the importance of leadership skills.

THE COMMON LEADERSHIP PROBLEM

I have spent countless hours training people worldwide to increase their leadership intelligence and make a greater difference in their sphere of influence. I would help people awaken their leadership potential, aid them in developing their leadership skills, and inspire them with divine possibilities to impact the world in a new and HUGE way.

Interestingly, I ran into the same problems and roadblocks over and over again. Leaders would start developing the teams necessary, become better coaches, and see amazing momentum and growth; however, at a certain point my clients would hit an invisible iron curtain and stop dead in their tracks. Why? Because *they didn't have enough of the necessary resources* to see additional breakthroughs.

When you believe you have unlimited potential and greatness inside you, the challenge you will have throughout your life is that your God-sized dreams will always be bigger than your current resources. Yet, God promises an abundant and unlimited supply of resources for every good work.

And God is able to make all grace [every favor and earthly blessing] come in abundance to you, so that you may always [under all circumstances, regardless of the need] have complete sufficiency in everything [being completely self-sufficient in Him], and have an abundance for every good work and act of charity (2 Corinthians 9:8 AMP).

Andy Frisella, CEO of 1st Phorm says, "Your biggest problem as an entrepreneur is getting the *resources* necessary to make your vision a reality."

I have coached people for years with a principle my mentor Bobb Biehl taught me: "As a leader you need to know:

- *What* to do next (priorities),

- *Why* it's important (purpose), and

- *How* to get the resources necessary (plan) to make what you want to do possible."

The person in any organization who knows the answers to these three things is the actual leader. If nobody can answer these three questions, there is no leader at the helm. A nice guy? Sure. A hard worker? Maybe. But a leader? Nope. After years of helping people develop their potential, I now can easily bring clarity to each person's individual situation about what to do next and why it's important.

The greatest challenge has always been the third point: How to get the person to start thinking abundantly, grasp the resources necessary, and then make a strategic plan of action.

LIVING WEALTHY MINDSET

IT'S NOT A LACK OF **RESOURCES**, BUT A LACK OF **RESOURCEFULNESS** THAT PREVENTS YOU FROM REACHING THE TARGET.

In a hotel room in Singapore, I realized that a fourth quotient is necessary for people and leaders to truly maximize their full potential—the Wealth Quotient (WQ). You might be thinking, *What does my Wealth Quotient (wealth intelligence) mean?*

Wealth Quotient is your belief and conviction that you are willing, worthy, and capable of creating, multiplying, maintaining, and distributing abundant resources necessary to serve millions of people with a determined effort to meet needs and solve problems.

WHAT EXACTLY IS WEALTH?

Wealth is a blessing to be embraced, not a curse to be rejected. Solomon said, "The blessing of the Lord brings wealth, without painful toil for it" (Proverbs 10:22 NIV). The word "rich" in the Hebrew language means "an accumulation of steadily growing wealth." (I like that. *Steadily* growing wealth.)

The word "wealth" comes from the Old English word *wela*, combined with the Middle English word *welth*, meaning "happiness and prosperity in abundance," and "well-being," respectively.

When we say the word "wealth," most people's minds go instantly toward money and material possession. But let me assure you this word is so much more expansive than having a lot of money or material possessions. Although I want you to know unequivocally that it's a very important part of the pie, it's not all of the pie. Your total, holistic well-being is.

Henry David Thoreau puts it this way, "Wealth is the ability to fully experience life." For all intents and purposes, I define wealth as maximizing your potential in all areas of your life. In fact, we will be discussing six different areas and a plan to increase your potential in those areas.

HIGH LEVELS OF WEALTH INTELLIGENCE (WQ) MEANS:

- You have plenty of **SPIRITUAL** encounters with God, so your spirit is energized and empowered to function at your full God-given potential.

- You have plenty of quality **RELATIONSHIPS** to support you, care for you, connect you, and work for you at building a dream.

- You have plenty of good **HEALTH** to overcome inertia and climb your mountain of great achievement.

- You have plenty of understanding, knowledge, and wisdom in your **MIND** to make the best decisions.

- You have plenty of developed talent and skill sets to operate in your **PROFESSION** at world-class levels in the growing global environment.

- You have plenty of **MONEY** or valuables to live a wealthy lifestyle, function in your purpose, confirm God's covenant in the earth, solve any problems you face, buy property or tools needed, hire the right people, help the masses, and fulfill your God-given assignment.

Many supposed "gurus" share a secret "key" to obtaining wealth. I hate to break the news to you, but there isn't a key. A key implies if you learn one script, one skill, and one strategy, you too can soon be sleeping on stacks of cash like Scrooge McDuck. Sorry. It doesn't work that way. I can assure you that key doesn't exist.

What *does* exist is a combination of confidences that lead to wealth. With these confidences, you can maximize your potential in six crucial areas of your life. Creating a life truly full of plenty and abundance.

I call these six areas of life: Six Wealth Combinations. The combinations to possessing a high WQ and to true wealth is a result of being healthy:

- Spiritually
- Mentally
- Relationally
- Professionally
- Physically
- Financially

Let me explain this from a holistic point of view with this illustration that we will be using throughout the book.

Each of these components of wealth are equally important and interconnected. As with any combination lock, if you miss stopping at one of these crucial points, you will block access to your potential.

Poverty or a lack of resources is the result of broken relationships in one or more of those six combinations. Wealth is the result of *healthy* interaction between all Six Wealth Combinations and is a sign of possessing a high WQ.

LIVING WEALTHY MINDSET

THERE IS NO SINGLE SOLUTION TO WEALTH. IT'S A COMBINATION, NOT A KEY, THAT UNLOCKS GOD'S UNLIMITED RESOURCES FOR YOUR LIFE.

Before we get too wrapped up in thinking that generating wealth is all about us, let's remember what Jesus, the Creator of the Universe, Son of God, the brightest and richest Man in the room, said: "The Son of Man came to serve, not to be served, and to give His life a ransom for many" (Matthew 20:28 plus see Philippians 2). This is how God the Son carried Himself, in humility serving the masses. This is His reality of wealth.

For all people and organizations to thrive today, they must think about positively impacting both locally and globally. We have to strategize how we can serve and provide more value to more people throughout the entire world.

LIVING WEALTHY MINDSET

YOUR WEALTH IS DETERMINED IN DIRECT PROPORTION TO THE VALUE YOU DELIVER TO THE MASSES IN THE MARKETPLACE.

The mark of true wealth is determined by how much one can give away. –T. Harv Eker, Best-Selling Author of *The Millionaire Mind*

WHO IS IT ABOUT?

I remember years ago meeting a pastor at one of my annual leadership meetings in Tampa, Florida. He was an older, average-looking guy, a little overweight, had a strong Southern accent, and I could tell during the conversation with him that his IQ was average. After the conference, the pastor invited me to come speak at his rural country church. I politely, yet hesitantly, accepted.

I will never forget the Sunday morning I showed up for the church service. The church wasn't little. It was a mega-size church out in the middle of nowhere. There were multiple, packed-out, simultaneous services in the sanctuary, gym, and the youth room. The entire time I was there I kept scratching my head thinking, *How is he able to pull this off?*

During lunch I finally had to ask him what the secret was to the large attendance. He said, "It's real simple, Keith, it's all about our mission statement. It's only one word—OTHERS!" What a simple but profound statement that leads to success.

The motto of the high achiever is, "What you make happen for others, God will make happen for you."

Zig Ziglar was famous for constantly saying, "You can have anything you want in life if you're willing to help other people get what they want in life." Ephesians 6:8 (NIV) reveals this same secret: "**The Lord will reward each one for whatever good they do**, whether they are slave or free."

You're probably thinking, *This sounds great, but how does this apply to me on a practical level?*

BASIC APPLICATIONS

The following are a few basic applications to consider:

- Create a service business that creates hundreds if not thousands of jobs to serve your local community and the masses.
- Create great products that the masses need or use.
- Build apartment buildings to house families.
- Use social media to add inspirational and informational value to the masses.

- Assist and educate others on how to discover their gifts, talents, and dreams.

It's incredible what happens when we shift our focus from self, to wealth. The Bible gives us some strong examples from which to glean truth and wisdom.

Job was the wealthiest man in the East, but in a moment lost everything. For a season he started focusing on himself and asking all the wrong questions. However, his life instantly changed when he started applying the WQ Combination, when he started praying for his friends. At the end of his crisis, he received double for all his trouble.

When a widow fed a tired prophet with her last meal, she received help when her dying son was healed (1 Kings 17).

Another very wealthy man of the Bible, Isaac had a WQ mindset for feeding, serving, and helping the masses. During a terrible famine, he decided to plant seed into the ground to grow food so he would have plenty, plus be able to provide food for others in the region.

Isaac planted crops in that land and the same year reaped a hundredfold, because the Lord blessed him. **The man became rich, and his wealth continued to grow until he became very wealthy.** He had so many flocks and herds and servants that the Philistines envied him (Genesis 26:12-14 NIV).

As the church, we need to ask ourselves, "What are the greatest problems and deepest needs felt by human beings?"

The wealthy person who faces this question at a gut level will go through an evolution of change in the mindset, strategy, style, branding, and spirit of their business and ministry—and will flourish, prosper, and touch the masses.

It's time for you to break through the final wall of resistance holding you back from achieving your dreams by learning the Six Wealth Combinations.

CHAPTER 4

SPIRITUAL WEALTH CONFIDENCE

DIVINE ADVANTAGES AND OPPORTUNITIES FOR SUCCESS

G OD HAS ALREADY DECIDED YOUR FUTURE spiritual, mental, professional, physical, and economic state. His desire for you is to be wealthy: "But remember the Lord your God, for it is he who gives you the ability to produce wealth" (Deuteronomy 8:18 NIV).

Growing in the six areas of the Wealth Quotient is no longer about "God deciding." He has already decided. It's now in your hands. You decide. You have to accept the gift of responsibility and ownership God has given you—and do something about it.

Your path to Living Wealthy requires a combination, a mixture of tools, insights, strategies, philosophies, and formulas. Within the next few chapters, you will discover how to grow in each one of these areas. We begin with growing your Spiritual Wealth.

It's important you recognize and acknowledge that God is the "Secret Sauce" to Living Wealthy. He gives you a positive, divine advantage. The ultimate "Secret Sauce" to success.

King Uzziah understood how to exploit the reality of God bestowing wealth: "As long as he sought the Lord, God made him prosper" (2 Chronicles 26:5).

Joseph also learned how God can make a person successful, despite his brothers' strategy to cause him to fail:

The Lord was with Joseph, and he [even though a slave] became a **successful and prosperous man**; and he was in the house of his master, the Egyptian (Genesis 39:2 AMP).

LIVING WEALTHY MINDSET

MONEY MAGNIFIES; IT DOESN'T MEDICATE.

When people lack a relationship with God, there will always be a void, a feeling of lack, that there is something missing in their lives. Building a financial empire, climbing the corporate ladder, job promotions, or accumulating great riches will actually heighten and accentuate the emptiness, rather than fill it.

LIVING WEALTHY MINDSET

YOUR SPIRITUALITY IS EITHER A BUCKET OF GAS ON THE FIRE OF YOUR WEALTH OR A BUCKET OF WATER THAT EXTINGUISHES THE FLAME.

When I speak to spiritual people, I find myself teaching the pragmatic principles to achieving success in life and creating wealth in order to achieve their dreams. And when I speak to business people, I find myself teaching about the importance of spirituality.

In seminars I often jokingly say, "When I was 23 years old, I was a professional sinner. If you're going to be something in life, don't be an amateur, be a world-class pro." I worked all day long to earn money so I could party all night long.

FILLING THE VOID

But during that time, God exposed me to some things that would eventually change my life. I worked in an environment full of financially wealthy people who wore several thousand-dollar Bespoke suits and alligator shoes, Rolex watches, and wrote with thousand-dollar Montblanc pens.

This was a new world for me. I was raised in abject poverty. In elementary school, I had to steal pencils and Bic pens because my parents couldn't afford school supplies. To think people had pens or other writing instruments that cost $300–$20,000 came as a shock to this ol' country boy.

Consequently, I wanted all the bling, bells, and whistles that make a person look rich. Making money all day and partying all night was my entire pursuit in life, yet I was determined to do whatever it took to fulfill my selfish desires. I was living that classic KISS song, "I want to rock and roll all night, and party every day!"

I had several "religious people" approach me at work and say, "You need to get your life right with God. You need to go to church." Of course, I didn't want anything to do with them. I was proud of being one of the best producers in the company. I looked down on them because they were actually some of the worst.

While they were huddled in the corner of the office praying for a successful day and reading the Bible, I was hustling and closing their sales. When I looked at their lives, I classified all Christians into three categories:

1. Broke and lazy. (I didn't want to be broke and I wasn't lazy.)

2. Nerds. (I was too good-looking to be a nerd.)

3. Unhappy. (I wanted to have fun.)

It didn't help that in almost every church I ever attended, I heard that pride was something to be shunned and condemned. Because I had pride in myself and my professional skills, I felt like a sinner every time I attended church. So, I started to hate myself *and* the church more and more.

RELIGION VERSUS CHRISTIANITY

Religion has contributed to many people's lack of confidence today. It's important to distinguish between *positive* pride and *negative* pride. Negative pride is that sense of arrogance that boasts, "I can do everything all by myself." It is the exact opposite of humility.

Positive pride is the confidence Jesus inspires us toward when He said, "Very truly I tell you, whoever believes in me will do the works I have been doing, and they will do even greater things than these" (John 14:12 NIV). The apostle Paul embodied this when he said, "I can do all things through Christ who strengthens me" (Philippians 4:13).

One Sunday morning I decided to attend a modern, vibrant church—and I heard the real message of the Gospel for the very first time. It was simple: "God loves you. Jesus came to die in your place and to forgive you of all your sins. God's grace can wipe away all your *guilt and shame* from all the wrong you did throughout your entire life. God will not remember your past from this day forward. I have good news, all you have to do is believe in Jesus Christ. Your life can change for the better starting today."

The "guilt and shame" statement really caught my attention, because I was feeling a lot of guilt and shame over the bad things that came with my past. Then the pastor quoted this Scripture from the Gospel of Matthew:

> For what profit is it to a man if he gains the whole world, and loses his own soul? Or what will a man give in exchange for his soul? (Matthew 16:26)

Wow! I thought, *He's talking to me! I've been chasing money like a butterfly I can never catch.* To be honest, I probably would have sold my soul for a BMW at the time if someone would have offered it to me. But after hearing the true word of God, I surrendered to God's promptings, humbled myself, and decided to give my life to Jesus Christ.

BAM! It happened! Something snapped inside me that I could not fully explain. I didn't want to do the things I used to do. I stopped going to bars, smoking, doing drugs, and chasing women. I started attending church weekly, praying daily, and reading the number one success book of all time—the Bible. That happened more than 25 years ago, and I've never looked back.

LIVING WEALTHY MINDSET

YOU ARE A SPIRITUAL CREATURE WHOSE DEEPEST NEEDS CAN ONLY BE MET AND SATISFIED ON A SPIRITUAL LEVEL.

Without a proper understanding of your Spiritual Wealth, you will continue to bump up against an invisible glass ceiling, limiting your Wealth Quotient and causing you to remain stuck where you are in life. Now I want to reveal to you the top three spiritual wealth deterrents:

1. The negative power of shame
2. The heavy load of guilt
3. The personal loss of identity

In addition to these deterrents are three wealth destroyers that work against you:

1. **Indecision.** You must have a hunger, desire, and drive to decide, to choose to become wealthy and increase your Wealth Quotient. What is the major difference between the rich and the poor? The rich choose to become rich, and the poor never make that decision.

2. **Unworthiness.** If you don't believe that you are worthy to receive wealth, there are people ready and willing to destroy your dignity and sense of value. You deserve it, not because of what you have done, but because of what God has promised.

3. **Inability.** You must have confidence in your ability to advance in life. "I don't think I can" rises from the deeper, "I don't think I am" attitude. The pain of inadequate ability destroys your potential.

Remember, the most powerful opposing forces on earth are confidence and shame.

In Genesis 2:17, we read that God made a supremely confident man in His own image and after His own likeness. In Genesis 2:25, we discover one of the key attributes of a thriving spiritual life that God gave humans to unleash their God-given potential in the earth: "And they were both naked, the man and his wife, and they were **not ashamed**."

The negative, destructive force of shame isn't revealed until after the fall of humankind, when the gap begins to widen in the confidence of the relationship between humanity and their Creator.

So he [Adam] said, "I heard Your voice in the garden, and I was afraid because I was naked; and I hid myself" (Genesis 3:10).

SHAME'S IMPACT ON FINANCIAL WEALTH

My own shame stripped me of confidence and caused me to do what Adam did in his shame. I hid myself by covering up my financial crisis for years. Who could I go to when I appeared to my family, friends, next door neighbors, and peers as if I was doing well financially, but really I was sinking in the quicksand of debt? Who could I go to when I was the supposed man of God, the business owner, when financial pressures came? Shame tells us that we can't trust anybody and people will think less of us if they know we're in trouble.

LIVING WEALTHY MINDSET

EXPOSURE IS TRANSFORMATIONAL AND SUPPLIES THE CONFIDENCE TO BEGIN AGAIN. SHAME PUTS YOU IN BONDAGE, BUT TRUTH SETS YOU FREE.

So I kept hiding my financial crisis, and credit cards helped me keep the covers on.

I will never forget the humiliation I felt when I sought a professional to help me get my finances straightened out. I had to pull back the covers and let him see all the years of lies and deception I had hoped nobody would ever find out about.

To my surprise, he applauded me for my boldness to face the facts. *Shame hates exposure.* When I pulled back the covers and exposed the mess, I instantly felt a weight lift off my shoulders. Then suddenly, the solutions on how to dig out of the hole started to appear.

Shame has no economic prejudices. Shame and guilt will make you feel bad about yourself when you are poor, but also tries to make wealthy people feel bad when they have an abundance of money.

In elementary school, I was always ashamed that I had to wear jeans from Kmart. Yet, a rich friend of mine intentionally dressed in ripped jeans and dirty T-shirts because he was ashamed of his parents' wealth.

——— LIVING WEALTHY MINDSET ———

SHAME AND GUILT ARE THE PLAGUES OF SPIRITUAL POVERTY, BUT CONFIDENCE IN GOD IS THE CURE THAT LEADS TO **LIVING WEALTHY.**

SHAME'S IMPACT ON YOUR PROFESSIONAL WEALTH

Adam and Eve thought they weren't good enough to be near God, so they hid. Shame is the curtain we hide behind when we feel inadequate and undeserving. It's a powerful force. In fact, it often feels better to use our shame to keep us from taking action than to bear the burden of possible failure. When you don't think you are good enough, you won't attempt something you've never done before.

Your true potential is discovered when you have the confidence to try something new. You will never discover your full potential until there is a demand placed on it.

When something new, an opportunity, presents itself in your professional field, confidence causes you to arise, step up, and accept the challenge because you know God is on your side and you can do it.

SHAME'S IMPACT ON YOUR RELATIONAL WEALTH

Shame's ugly head prevents you from developing better relationships. In the same way shame disconnected Adam and Eve from a relationship with God, if not dealt with, shame can keep us from connecting with the people who can help us get to where we want to go in life.

Shame prevents you from thinking that you are worthy of associating with people of a higher status. Therefore, your Relational Wealth

47

will be poor. Confidence says, "Nobody is better than me, and I am not better than others. I belong in the presence of greatness."

SHAME'S IMPACT ON PHYSICAL WEALTH

God wanted humankind to live forever; however, Genesis 5:5 reveals the end result of shame: "So all the days that Adam lived were nine hundred and thirty years; and he died."

David R. Hawkins, MD, PhD, is a renowned psychiatrist and scientist who spent a good portion of his life studying the connection between human emotions and the body. In his book *Power vs. Force,* he reveals how emotion affects the physical body. Dr. Hawkins found that guilt and shame are the two most destructive emotions a human can experience—they actually weaken the physical body.[1]

Hawkins' studies concluded that the most powerful emotions a human can experience are peace, joy, and love—and these emotions empower the physical body with great strength.

For the Kingdom of God is not a matter of what we eat and drink, but of living a life of goodness and peace and joy in the Holy Spirit (Romans 14:17 New Living Translation).

SHAME'S IMPACT ON MENTAL WEALTH

When Adam was questioned by God about why he ate from the forbidden tree, Adam blamed his wife. Shame-based people are so insecure and mentally weak that they don't have the confidence to take responsibility or ownership for their actions. Shame and blame are siblings. Shame always blames somebody or something else.

I used to blame everybody for what was wrong in my life. Instead of accepting my responsibility, I shifted the blame to God, the devil, my spouse, my upbringing, my boss, the government, the economy, and anything else I could justify in my mind.

During my financial crisis, when we were living with my mother-in-law, I remember walking out the door and going toward my car. I looked up to the sky and yelled, "WHAT'S STOPPING ME?" I opened the car door, jumped in, and turned on the radio. Surprisingly, there was a prophet singing. I turned up the volume. His name was Michael Jackson.

What?! you may be wondering. Yes, at that point in time, he was a prophet who answered my question when he sang, "I'm starting with the man in the mirror, I'm asking him to change his ways."

LIVING WEALTHY MINDSET

TAKING 100 PERCENT **RESPONSIBILITY** FOR THE CONDITION OF YOUR LIFE IS THE FIRST STEP TO BUILDING REAL WEALTH. THE SECOND STEP IS TO TAKE **OWNERSHIP** OF YOUR CONDITION BY DOING WHATEVER IT TAKES TO CHANGE IT.

For years, I heard pastors say, "You need to have a little talk with Jesus." However, I discovered I needed to have a *serious* talk with myself. When I returned home that evening, I locked myself in the bathroom, looked right into the mirror, and let myself have it. I accepted responsibility for the financial mess, my pride, and for all I had done that I knew was wrong and blamed someone else for. What a relief! I felt like a new man—a man of integrity, a man who could change the world, one act of forgiveness at a time from my heavenly Father.

So let me ask you, have you dealt with the person in the mirror lately?

SHAME ATTACKS YOUR CONFIDENCE WITH NEGATIVE SELF-TALK

When I speak, I often ask the crowd, "How many of you have had people say some really negative things about you?" Of course, everybody raises their hands. Then I say, "Nobody has talked more negatively about you than YOU!"

You cannot build internal wealth by continuing to demonize yourself over your present and past behaviors or failures. If you don't forgive yourself, you will continue to think you deserve to be punished and will subconsciously do bad things to yourself to sabotage your future success and limit your wealth.

Psychologists have discovered that for every 10 minutes of negativity you hear, you need 100 minutes of something positive to erase those thoughts from your subconscious mind. I spent one year renewing my mind by meditating on the following Scriptures to erase the effects of negative self-talk.

There is therefore now no condemnation to those who are in Christ Jesus, who do not walk according to the flesh, but according to the Spirit (Romans 8:1).

If we confess our sins, He is faithful and just to forgive us our sins and to cleanse us from all unrighteousness (1 John 1:9).

As far as the east is from the west, so far has He removed our transgressions from us (Psalm 103:12).

LIVING WEALTHY MINDSET

TURN YOUR INNER CRITIC INTO AN INNER COACH. GOD DOESN'T CONSULT YOUR PAST TO DETERMINE YOUR FUTURE.

SHAME AND GUILT'S IMPACT ON YOUR SPIRITUAL WEALTH

Shame says, "I'm ashamed of who I am." Shame can be difficult to overcome because it attacks who you are, not what you do. Shame always leaves you feeling like you are a bad person and that you are the problem. This is the feeling many people who have been sexually abused experience. The perpetrators leave their victims feeling like it's their fault.

Guilt says, "I feel bad about what I have done." Guilt says that our behavior or actions are bad. Guilt can be healthy because it lets us know we have violated our personal values. When we do something wrong, guilt tells us that we need to go back and fix it.

If you don't forgive yourself, the guilt for your wrong behaviors can move into the toxic emotions of shame. Then your mind goes from, *I feel bad about what I've done* to the garbage dump of thinking, *I'm such a bad person.*

Jesus hates what the negative power of shame does to humanity. He hates shame so much that He willingly took on our shame so we can be totally forgiven and shame-free: "for the joy that was set before Him [Jesus] endured the cross, despising the shame" (Hebrews 12:2).

LIVING WEALTHY MINDSET

GUILT AND SHAME KEEP YOU ON THE TEETER TOTTER OF PERFORMANCE-BASED LOVE, BUT CONFIDENCE IN THE PERFECT LOVE OF GOD IS THE GREAT EQUALIZER.

God has forgiven and forgotten your past. Now it's time to forgive yourself. The only person who can continue to condemn you is you. Break that cycle now!

YOUR TRUE IDENTITY

The disciples wanted to learn how to pray. Jesus taught them a prayer that would forever release them from the crippling forces of insecurity and demoralizing power of guilt and shame. He revealed to them their true identity.

LIVING WEALTHY MINDSET

GOD DOESN'T DESIRE SLAVES AND SERVANTS. HE WANTS SONS AND DAUGHTERS.

For centuries it's been referred to as The Lord's Prayer, but I call it The Confidence Prayer.

Jesus deals with our shame, guilt, and *identity* issues from the outset when He begins the prayer with, "**Our Father** in heaven" (Matthew 6:9). Please note, Jesus didn't begin the prayer with, "Our Cynic, Critic, or Cop." Sadly, most people see God as a stern police officer instead of our ultimate coach.

Rather, God is our loving Father. We are His children. We are members of His divine, royal family. It's His name on the back of our jersey, not some football or basketball player. That should be our confidence. The good news of the Gospel is that we are now identified with God's family.

The Confidence Prayer calls us to this affirmation: "I know who I am! God is my Father! I am His child. I am somebody. I bear His honorable name. I am loved. I am valuable. I am forgiven. I am completely and unconditionally accepted by my Father."

ENDNOTE

1. David R. Hawkins, MD, PhD, *Power vs. Force* (Carlsbad, CA: Hay House, Inc., 2014), 68-69.

CHAPTER 5

MENTAL WEALTH CONFIDENCE

THE COMMAND CENTER OF YOUR CREATIVE POWERS

GOD THE CREATOR MADE YOU UNIQUE and gave you a very valuable asset—your mind. With your mind you have the ability to choose and make decisions that create and shape your future. Decisions ultimately decide your wealth.

So, one of your greatest assets for creating a Living Wealthy lifestyle is your mind. The greatest logical investment should be in adding value to your mind. To become a wealthy person, you must start thinking wealthy like God. That's what Proverbs 4:7 tells us when it says getting wisdom is the wisest thing we can do. We need to learn to think like God.

Let's take a moment and consider what makes us different from a bird, elephant, fish, flower, or the moon and stars? Without a doubt, the Creator gave the human race the unique capacity and the ability to *think*.

```
┌───────────── LIVING WEALTHY MINDSET ─────────────┐
│   YOUR MIND'S GREATEST RESOURCE IS YOUR          │
│   GOD-LIKE CREATIVE POWER OF IMAGINATION.        │
└───────────────────────────────────────────────────┘
```

With our minds we have been given the amazing ability to imagine. Your *imagination* gives you the ability to quickly and instantly create images in your mind based on your five senses:

1. Hearing
2. Smell
3. Touch
4. Taste
6. Sight

Imagining is the ability of the mind to be creative and resourceful. The action of forming new ideas, solutions, images, and pictures of future events not currently present.

```
┌───────────── LIVING WEALTHY MINDSET ─────────────┐
│   WHAT YOU PICTURE IN YOUR MIND OVER             │
│   TIME BECOMES A PREVIEW TO YOUR FUTURE          │
│           COMING ATTRACTIONS.                     │
└───────────────────────────────────────────────────┘
```

When you go to the movies, the 15 minutes prior to the show is filled with previews of movies that will be released in the future. Our imaginations can do the same thing in that we can imagine what we want to see, do, plan, etc. in the future—then we can make it happen, if we choose to do so.

I want you to say out loud, "pink elephant." Did you say it? Do it now! Say out loud, "pink elephant." Now, did you see a pink elephant in your mind? Yes. Of course you did. Is there such a thing as a pink elephant? No. But you created one with your imagination.

Unfortunately, I really didn't understand the power of imagination until my late 30s after I had achieved a certain degree of success. I was stuck going through the motions of my daily routines, doing what I had to do to keep the business running. I wasn't letting my imagination of the future pull me; I was letting the rut of routine restrict me.

COACHES STRETCH YOUR MENTAL LIMITATION

I realized that I needed a coach. Someone to come alongside and challenge me to my core. I was in a mental fog and needed *clarity and direction.*

The first session with my newly hired coach started with this question: "What does the picture of your future look like over the next 10 years of your life?" Ten years?! To be honest, it was hard for me to see beyond next week. So I started quoting my yearly Christian clichés. I'm sure you've heard these before. "This is going to be a year of favor. This is the year of breakthrough, this is the year of divine turnaround. This is the year of blah, blah, blah."

My coach's transformational reply: "Keith, your first problem is that you're thinking way too small. Small thinking creates small motivation. Why are you just thinking one year? Why don't you think in decades? Why don't you use your imagination and dream as if the next decade is going to be the best decade of your entire life?"

LIVING WEALTHY MINDSET
WHAT IS SEEABLE IS BELIEVABLE, AND WHAT IS BELIEVABLE BECOMES ACHIEVABLE.

When you start thinking like God thinks, without limitations, generationally and futuristically, your level of motivation will increase. More intense motivation causes you to take massive action to create new and grander results in your life. You are motivated to become what you imagine yourself to be. You begin to demand more of your future self.

Being immersed in church culture for more than two decades had conditioned me to think yearly instead of futuristically. One study found that the super wealthy think years in advance, the middle class

55

tend to think only to the end of the week or pay period, and the poor tend to think about the next hour or how to satisfy immediate needs.

Comedian George Burns, at 99 years of age, had the foresight to sign a 10-year contract with Caesars Palace. He said he was going to demand a 20-year contract, but didn't think they would be in business that long. Now that's forward thinking!

God gave you an imagination to be able to create. Before God created everything, He saw it in His imagination before He spoke it into existence. Everything He created was in the mind of God before it became a reality. How? God used His imagination. Remember, God created us in His own likeness and in His own image, and God gave us a tool, our imagination, an image maker.

You have the ability to create these images of Living Wealthy in your mind. The animals, flowers, and sun have the ability to produce, but they don't have the ability to imagine and produce something that has never been created before. A flower can reproduce another flower, but it can't create a greenhouse. A fish can reproduce another fish, but it can't create a fishing boat. The sun can produce light, but it can't create a solar panel.

Everything created was actually created twice. Once in the invisible with the mind and then in the physical. Everything ever created started as a picture generated by someone's imagination.

Your imagination is what gives you "God-like" powers to create. This is what makes you a superior creation and separates you from the sun, moon, plants, animals, and even angels and demons.

FIRE UP THE IMAGINATION FACTORY

It's about time to awaken and activate your imagination. God has already given you everything you need to be successful. With the right tools, success can be a lot easier than you think. Tools help you accelerate the process and your progress. However, unused tools make your progress slow and harder than necessary.

Activate your imagination to create a 10x vision. The purpose of your imagination is to play the movie preview of your potential future. You can never tap into your full potential unless you can imagine accomplishing something unusual in your future. Walt Disney imagined a huge theme park where families could go to enjoy wholesome entertainment and fun—a place where people could escape the hustle and bustle of life. Disney said, "If you can dream it, you can do it."

The Bible story of the Tower of Babel is a powerful illustration of how God Himself said humankind can achieve anything by harnessing imagination. Genesis 11:6 in the King James Version reads, "and now nothing will be restrained from them, which they have **imagined** to do."

LIVING WEALTHY MINDSET

YOUR IMAGINATION KNOWS NO LIMITS. IF YOUR IMAGINATION IS LIMITLESS, THEN SO IS YOUR POTENTIAL.

Your imagination is the most powerful ingredient of change formation in your life. A change of season demands a change of pictures of what you see happening to you in the Six Areas of Living Wealthy.

Imagine what is possible over the next *decade* of your life. I don't want you to just have a great year, but a great *10 years!* Imagine your life ten times bigger and better than what you are experiencing now. Think about what's possible with your imagination in each of these areas:

- **Spiritually** - Think about your contribution to the world getting 10x greater.
- **Mentally** - Think about your decisions growing 10x wiser.
- **Physically** - Think about your physical shape being 10x healthier.
- **Relationally** - Think about the quality of your relationships getting 10x richer.
- **Professionally** - Think about your marketplace influence becoming 10x more impactful.
- **Financially** - Think about your income growing 10x richer.

My job as a coach is to pull out the potential that's already inside you—to challenge you and show you that your life could be better, bigger, and brighter than your life today. In order for me to do that, you need to use your imagination to look beyond now and see the divine possibilities waiting for you to embrace.

```
┌─────────────── LIVING WEALTHY MINDSET ───────────────┐
│                                                       │
│   YOUR CURRENT REALITY DOESN'T HAVE TO                │
│   BECOME YOUR FUTURE DESTINY. WHAT YOU                │
│   SEE IN YOUR MIND BECOMES TRUE IN TIME.             │
│                                                       │
└───────────────────────────────────────────────────────┘
```

LIMITING BELIEFS = IMAGINATION KRYPTONITE

Did you know it's possible to limit God? Yes, it is. When you limit your beliefs, your future, your organization, and your wealth, you can limit what God wants to do in your life. The Bible says that in the wilderness the children of Israel limited God with their small-minded thinking.

Yes, again and again they tempted God, and limited the Holy One of Israel (Psalm 78:41).

Taking your life up to the next level isn't difficult in the mind of God. Everything is easy for Him. "Behold, I am the Lord, the God of all flesh. Is there anything too hard for Me?" (Jeremiah 32:27).

STRONGHOLDS

When talking about your future, all your strongholds and psychological issues will come to the surface. Placing a demand on your potential forces all your wrong beliefs and small thinking to be revealed.

I spent many years in a spiritual warfare mentality of *pulling down strongholds.* I thought my job was to pull down demonic forces in the heavenly realms that had set themselves against me. My life started changing when I realized the strongholds were not necessarily in heaven, but were the thoughts in my own head!

For the weapons of our warfare are ... for ... casting down arguments (strongholds) and every high thing that exalts itself against the knowledge of God, **bringing every thought into captivity** to the obedience of Christ (2 Corinthians 10:5).

I was running into a stronghold, a belief system that is resistant to change.

There is a **Three-Step Process** that you will need to walk through in order to identify your current restraints and break through your current strongholds.

STEP 1 - LISTEN TO AND THEN DELETE YOUR "I CAN'T BECAUSE_____."

I have heard all kinds of stories about why people can't change their lives. "I can't because of my boss. I can't because there are no job opportunities. I can't because I don't have enough education." And, of course, the big one, "I can't because I don't have enough money."

All of these *reasons* are simply your imagination gone wild creating incorrect stories or mental movies about why it can't happen.

What is your *I Can't Because* story? Once you identify the story, all you have to do is simply stop listening to the self-limiting belief and write a new storyline, one of unlimited divine possibilities of how you *can* do it.

What is that story you keep playing in your head about why you can't achieve your dream? Identify the story, change the story, change your life.

STEP 2 - TURN ON THE POWER OF "I CAN BECAUSE _____!"

When you feed yourself the "I can" scenario, your mind is designed to produce the "how to." Now you are tapping into the "thinking like God" side of your imagination.

Your imagination is fueled by the belief that you can do it.

When you tell yourself "I can," your mind is designed by God to engage your imagination to be able to think outside of your currently perceived limitation so you can figure out ways to make your dreams come true.

Fuel the power of your imagination with the *I Can Because* mindset.

STEP 3 - IGNITE YOUR NEW "I WILL _____!" DECREE.

The next step is to take your "I *can* because _____" to "I *will* because _____." It's one thing to think or say you can; it's another thing to have the guts to take the action necessary to make it happen, no matter what it takes.

Your new decree should sound like this: "I will increase ten times every area of my life in the next 10 years. I will upgrade my skills by reading one hour every day. I will increase my income by ten times! I will save my first $100,000! I will give ten times more to reaching and helping more people."

You have to have that "I will no matter what it takes" mindset—as long as it's inside the laws of God.

ACTIVATING YOUR IMAGINATION TO DESIGN YOUR FUTURE

Your mind needs two things:

1. A PICTURE OF THE FUTURE.

Your mind needs a clear picture of who you want to be, what you want to do, what you want to have, and who you want to help in the future.

You must use your imagination to feed your mind with the picture. And you know what I find coaching people? Most people don't want to put the picture in their minds until they figure out "how" to do it. *You* are not responsible for the "how to." God is.

You are responsible to put the picture in your mind with your imagination and believe it's possible for you to make the picture a reality. Then God develops the how-to in your mind so you can start working toward figuring out how to make the believable picture possible.

This was the mistake I made prior to my move to my mother-in-law's house. I was waiting for God to do for me what God was expecting me to do.

```
┌──────────── LIVING WEALTHY MINDSET ────────────┐
│     WE ARE CO-CREATORS WITH GOD IN THE          │
│              GRACE OF LIFE.                      │
└─────────────────────────────────────────────────┘
```

2. A PICTURE OF A HERO.

Your mind needs a clear picture of a hero. A person you want to become in the future. Some people get all religious and say, "Well, my hero is Jesus!"

Great! You can have Jesus as your hero, but you must also find a person who is ten times further along in life and currently doing what you want to be doing. Then model the person, research the person, find out all you can about the person. Success leaves clues. Study that person. Read the books and blogs. Watch the YouTube channel. Consume all the data the person writes and creates.

Learn how the person does it. Then do what your hero does and you'll experience the same, or better, success. As you become successful, you'll eventually evolve into the person you are supposed to become.

Let's look at some well-known examples:

- Kobe Bryant's hero was Michael Jordan.
- Lady Gaga's hero was Whitney Houston.
- Oprah's hero was Barbara Walters.
- Mike Tyson's hero was Muhammad Ali.

Each of these examples modeled their mentor until they evolved into themselves. When I was in my mother-in-law's house, I wondered, *Who's going to be my hero?* For me it was John Maxwell.

I wanted to speak and train people about leadership in churches and in business. So I followed John, I studied him, I learned from him, and I did what he did. I modeled what he did, became successful, and then I evolved into my own person.

YOUR GOD-DESIGNED MIND

Has this ever happened to you? When you consider buying a certain vehicle, all of a sudden it seems like everyone is driving that same car? Let's say you're looking at a Toyota Corolla. Why a Corolla? I don't know, I guess because it's the #1 selling car of all time. This is just an example.

Anyway, suddenly it seems like this car is everywhere! You never noticed before, but your neighbor has one. You pass three or four Corollas on your drive to work. You pull in at work and there are a few more. On your drive home that evening you count six more!

What happened? Is this a sign from God? Did everyone decide to buy a Toyota Corolla at the same exact time? No. You're experiencing a function of your reticular activating system (RAS).

Throughout this chapter you have read how God created your mind to be a command center for your creative powers. This isn't just a mystical idea; it's also proven neurological science.

The RAS is a web of neurons in your brain stem and functions a lot like a search engine in your mind. You ask a question, present a problem or opportunity, and then it gets to work on a subconscious level, seeking a solution.

God wouldn't empower you with a wealth tool that gives you the incredible ability to imagine future accomplishments and conditions if you were not correspondingly equipped with the ability to turn those images into a reality.

God wants you to know that the only limitations you will ever face will be the ones you decide to place on yourself. Your potential exceeds way beyond what you can imagine (Ephesians 3:20).

Tai Lopez says we have to see possibilities before we pursue possibilities. I want to encourage you. What is your potential? Do you see it? When you lay your head down to sleep, imagine it. Play with the possibilities in your mind. Put your reticular activating system to work for you. Then awaken to a new reality.

CHAPTER 6

PHYSICAL WEALTH CONFIDENCE

ACTIONS AND MOTIONS REQUIRED TO MAINTAIN MOMENTUM

WHEN I WAS STUCK IN MY MOTHER-IN-LAW's house, I decided to take massive action toward making a huge difference in the world by speaking to one million people about the subject of confidence. I set a huge goal that I wanted to speak to a group of people 365 days of the year. Yes. I know. Really crazy goal. But really crazy goals do create at least crazy results that most people never experience.

I never hit my goal of speaking every day to a group of people, but I came very close. For 10 years straight, I was on the road speaking an average of 230 days of the year. I must admit, the demands on my body from years of eating while running through airports and late-night dinners with leaders eventually caught up to me.

During one of my speaking tours in South Africa, the dean of my college there noticed I was gasping for air during my speeches and I had gained a lot of weight. At the end of every message, I was soaked in perspiration and was exhausted. He advised me to seek medical advice.

After that trip I kept hearing a voice say, "Keith, if you are going to make it for the long haul, you need to get your physical body in peak shape." I knew it was time for a change, so I made a commitment that week to develop a new healthy lifestyle. This is the declaration I used to start seeing myself as a world-class athlete and went from 29 percent body fat all the way down to a lean 13 percent body fat.

LIVING WEALTHY MINDSET

THINK OF YOURSELF AS A WORLD-CLASS ATHLETE RUNNING TOWARD YOUR DESTINY. YOU WILL DAILY EXERCISE, STRETCH YOUR MUSCLES, EAT THE RIGHT FOODS, AND REST YOUR BODY.

Ask yourself this question, *Do I love myself enough to take care of my body?*

Imagine with me for a moment that I gave you a $10 million race horse. Now, let me ask you a few questions about this horse:

- Would you keep the horse locked up in the barn and never exercise it?

- Would you feed it candy bars, fast food, and junk food all day long?

- Would you take your horse out to party all night?

- Would you give it drugs or cigarettes every day?

Of course you wouldn't. Why not? Because of the great expense and value of your multimillion dollar gift from me. If you wouldn't treat a horse like that, why in the world would you treat yourself so badly?

The only logical answer is that you lack confidence and a positive self-esteem because you don't really value yourself and your body.

If your dog or cat is fat, you aren't getting enough exercise. If you really value yourself, you will take better care of your body. Low self-esteem is the root cause of obesity. –Dr. Oz

Your physical body is the temple or house in which God lives. "Do you not know that you are the temple of God and that the Spirit of God dwells in you?" (1 Corinthians 3:16). You need to take good care of your body because it is God's tool, which He uses to express Himself. God needs your body to be a channel that He uses to accomplish His will on earth. My body, your body, is the conduit through which divine activities are performed.

LIVING WEALTHY MINDSET

YOU CAN'T MAKE A SPIRITUAL IMPACT WITHOUT GREAT PHYSICAL HEALTH.

Richard Branson, billionaire entrepreneur, was asked, "What is key to building your business?" His reply, "My fitness." Your body needs to function at peak performance because in order to achieve your dream, you need one thing, ENERGY! The bigger the dream and the higher the desire you have to climb to the top, the more energy you need to do it.

LIVING WEALTHY REQUIRES ENERGY

During the 2016 Republican primary race, many believed that Governor Jeb Bush should have been the one elected to run for President of the United States. He had all of the obvious ingredients to win the vote: a family history in politics and all the connections that go with that privilege, the experience of being governor of Florida, the majority support of the Republican Party, and millions and millions of dollars in contributions.

However, Governor Bush lacked one thing, and his strongest opponent, Donald Trump, exposed it live on stage during a debate when he said, "Jeb, you're a low energy guy!" Everybody on stage and around the world laughed. Why? Because it was true. And Jeb instantly fell in the polls and never recovered. Jeb lost the opportunity of a lifetime to be the President of the United States.

Later, in the 2016 presidential election, the highly experienced and well-funded Hillary Clinton was touted to win the election, but she lost. Of course many people have different opinions as to why she lost, but there is a common denominator: energy.

Clinton didn't grant any television interviews for more than 200 days and only threw a few rallies in different states here and there. It appeared as though in the last few months of her run for office that her physical body didn't have the energy necessary to sustain and win the most important campaign of her life. Her lack of energy and good health culminated in a series of fainting spells leading up to the election.

On the other side of the aisle, Trump accepted every television interview he was available for and he hustled and pounded the trail, conducting multiple rallies in different states almost every day. Without a doubt, his energy level for a 70-year-old man was off the charts. At the end of the day, once again, the person with the most energy won the vote.

The number one asset a pastor, speaker, entrepreneur, business owner, or anybody must bring to work is energy. I jokingly tell leaders to do whatever they have to do to get energy. Drink four double shot cappuccinos or a couple of Red Bulls. But please don't come up on the stage without energy and excitement. Putting out energy places a demand on your physical body.

Take care of your body. It's the only place you have to live.
–Jim Rohn

YOUR PHYSIOLOGY IS A TOOL FOR WEALTH BUILDING

Experts in all fields are proving daily that physical, spiritual, mental, financial, professional, and emotional health are very closely tied together. You can't ignore one at the expense of the other. When one area isn't functioning in a wholesome manner, the other areas suffer.

Your physical body is another tool you have in your arsenal that can either empower you or render you powerless.

Physiology is the study of the functions of living organisms and their parts. Physiology deals with how you use your physical body for things like posture, breathing, smile, and movement.

Both your brain and your body work in harmony together to help you operate at peak levels of energy, that is, if you know how to use them. Your physiology communicates with your brain and tells it what to do, and then your brain communicates to the body and tells it what to do. Almost as instantly as the mind thinks something, there is an observable response in the physical body.

I like to use an illustration at my meetings to emphasize the mind and body connection. I ask someone from the audience to join me on stage. I ask him to hold his arm straight out to the side. I then push down on the arm and tell him to resist me.

Then I say, "Now, I want us to do the same thing, but I want you to remember a time in your life when you were at your peak, when you were doing your best. This time I want you to see in your imagination." Then I push down on the person's arm. I can hardly move it, even if I use all my strength.

Then I say, "Great job! You are very strong. Now, I want you to remember the worst day of your life. Can you remember? I want you to experience all the emotion you were feeling. See the picture of that day as clearly as you can."

The audience can see the physiology of the person instantly change. The head drops, the shoulders slump, and the arm being held out straight starts to fall naturally. Then with only two fingers, I can push the arm down with great ease.

What does this illustration teach us? What we think affects the strength and energy being released from the physical body. *Our psychology affects our physiology.*

Your physiology communicates to people more than your words and even your tone of voice. Words represent 7 percent of what actually influences human behavior. Voice qualities represent 38 percent of what influences another human being. How you use your voice affects someone more than what you say.

Physiology represents 55 percent. The way you use your body represents the majority of what actually influences people when you communicate.

```
┌──────────── LIVING WEALTHY MINDSET ────────────┐
│   YOU CAN CHANGE YOUR PSYCHOLOGY AND           │
│   YOUR EMOTIONAL STATE BY CHANGING YOUR        │
│              PHYSIOLOGY.                        │
└────────────────────────────────────────────────┘
```

Now let's do an experiment together. I want you to try an exercise for a moment. Slump your shoulders down. Now, hang your head down and add a frown on your face. Question: How do you feel?

Depressed?

Insecure?

Down on yourself?

Sad?

One of the easiest ways to develop confidence that attracts success is to change your physical posture.

Here's another quick exercise. Hold your head up straight and look forward. Stop looking at the ground because it causes your whole body to slump over. Pick a spot on the wall to look at that is slightly above your line of sight. Pull your shoulders back and stick out your chest. Add a nice smile on your face. How do you feel now?

Confident?

Important?

Secure?

Like a champion?

Here is a powerful thing to understand about yourself. If you did the exercise, you were able to change how you felt and instantly increase your energy levels without changing the way you think or stimulating yourself with outside sources like antidepressants, coffee, cigarettes, or drugs.

You simply changed your physiology, and your energy, emotions, and feelings instantly changed.

Now, hold your head up. Straighten your shoulders. Walk with an unstoppable, confident step, as if you had somewhere important to go. Use your physiology as a tool to change your psychology, and you can instantly change how you feel.

Emotion is the product of motion. The key to success is to create patterns of movement and posture that create confidence, a sense of strength, flexibility, power, and fun.

Have you ever gone on a cross-country drive that required you to be on the road late at night? I am really bad about falling asleep at the wheel, especially at night. What do you do when you start nodding off while driving? Have you ever slapped your face or just shook yourself? What happened? You experienced a quick boost of energy.

You did not change your thoughts nor did you say anything. You simply changed your physiology with motion and your energy levels increased and your mental and emotional state changed for the better.

NINE WAYS TO IMPROVE YOUR PHYSIOLOGY AND INCREASE ENERGY

1. WEAR YOUR MILLION-DOLLAR SMILE.

This is the quickest way to change the way you feel and boost your energy. It's almost impossible to smile on the outside and feel crummy on the inside. By the way, invest in your smile to make it look as nice as you can. Brush, floss, have your teeth cleaned twice a year, and whiten them if you need to. It's worth your investment.

2. SIT UP STRAIGHT.

Our culture today is based on entertainment. People watch up to 6 hours of television a day. What is your physiology when you watch TV? Kicked back. Relaxed. Usually slouching in a chair. You may be doing it right now as you read this book—sit up in your chair right now! Make this a habit.

It is said people can only focus for thirty minutes of learning. This is true when your audience is not totally engaged. In my weekend conferences, I teach students how to put themselves in a place where they can learn for hours at a time. If the student is totally engaged mentally and physically, there is no limit to how long a person can learn. Well, I mean as long as their butts can take it.

The simple act of sitting up in the seat causes your mind to be more alert and positioned to receive.

3. GIVE HUGS.

Psychologist Virginia Satir said that we need four hugs a day for survival, eight hugs a day for maintenance, and twelve hugs a day for growth. Just think, by simply giving a hug you can make someone instantly feel better. You did not change their psychology nor did you say a word. Your physiology changes their physiology with a simple hug. By the way, hugs have been proven to improve your immune system as well.

4. WALK FASTER.

Pick up your pace. Psychologists link a poor posture and slow, sluggish walking to a negative attitude toward oneself. People who know who they are and where they are going have pep in their step. They naturally walk faster. People who have had a rough life and seem to be going nowhere have a shuffle in their walk. Pick up your pace, and you will feel a pickup in your confidence. A hiring manager once told me that during his interview process, he asks his job candidates to take a walk with him. If the person can't keep up, he doesn't offer them a second interview.

No citizen has a right to be an amateur in the matter of physical training. What a disgrace it is for a man to grow old without ever seeing the beauty and strength of which his body is capable. –Socrates

5. MONITOR AND CONTROL YOUR BODY WEIGHT.

Gaining weight is something that happens to all of us. The average American gains at least one pound per year after the age of 25. That means by the time you're 50, you would have put on twenty-five pounds. In addition, your metabolism slows down. This causes the body to work less efficiently at burning the fat it has.

At the same time, if you don't exercise, you will lose one pound of muscle per year. Losing muscle slows down your metabolism even more, and also increases risk of injury and decreases activity performance. Weight gain happens by default. Health gain happens by design. Be intentional.

Nevertheless, I will bring health and healing to it; I will heal my people and will let them enjoy abundant peace and security (Jeremiah 33:6 NIV).

6. EAT FOR ENERGY.

Do not go on diets that have a name. They are marketing gimmicks, or at best, fads. As a matter of fact, don't go on a diet at all. Incorporate eating healthy as a lifestyle. Keep track of your calorie intake. Burn more calories than you eat. I'm amazed how thick most diet books are today.

My weight loss coaching tips are very easy: think better, eat less (junk), eat more (six small meals a day), move more. That's it. Do that with consistency and the needle on the scale will move backward.

7. EXERCISE YOUR WAY TO PEAK PERFORMANCE.

Physical fitness has a huge effect on self-confidence. If you're out of shape, you'll feel insecure, unattractive, and less energetic. By working out, you improve your physical appearance, energize yourself, and accomplish something positive. Having the discipline to work out not only makes you feel better, it creates positive momentum that you can build on throughout the rest of the day.

For physical training is of some value, but godliness (spiritual training) is of value in everything and in every way, since it holds promise for the present life and for the life to come (1 Timothy 4:8 AMP).

8. DRINK MORE WATER FOR ENERGY.

Do you ever get really tired about three o'clock in the afternoon? I used to. So I would take a nap and then wake up 15 minutes later feeling miserable. Or sometimes I would go to Starbucks and drink a high-octane coffee for fuel.

CONFIDENCE FOR LIVING WEALTHY

One day somebody told me to slam down an eight-ounce glass of water when I was feeling tired and my energy levels would increase. The next day, sure enough, around 3 p.m. I started feeling tired, so I drank a glass of water and went back to work. The next thing I knew, I was still working at 9 p.m.

Wow! I was sold on the idea that water equals energy. I realized I had been living in a dehydrated state. If you suffer from inadequate hydration, you may feel tired, hungry, bloated, and sluggish.

The importance of drinking the proper amount of water cannot be stressed enough if you really want to be your best and operate at your peak every day. The body simply can't adapt to dehydration, which impairs every function of the body. Studies show that fluid loss of even 2 percent of body weight will adversely affect circulatory functions and decrease performance levels.

LIVING WEALTHY MINDSET

TIRED PEOPLE LEAN TOWARD PROBLEMS.
RESTED PEOPLE LEAN TOWARD ANSWERS.

Every function, every organ, every cell in your body needs water to survive. Three out of four people today live in a dehydrated state.

If 85 percent of our brains and muscles contain water, how can we possibly be performing at our best if we are dehydrated? What would happen if you sucked all the juice out of a watermelon? It would totally shrivel up.

It is the same with the cells in your body. They need to be energized with water or they will not function at peak. But if you give your cells the fuel of water, they will respond by allowing your body to perform even better.

9. GOD AND LIONS DO THIS.

When fatigue walks in, faith and confidence walk out. It has been said that most people are operating with a two-hour sleep deficit. God worked 6 days and rested. If God Himself needed to rest, how much more does your mortal body need rest?

Here's an interesting thought. If you stumbled upon a lion in the afternoon, you would think he was lazy. No. Lions sleep all day and hunt at night. Whether you are creating the universe from thin air or hunting prey to feed your family, you need rest.

Sleep is all about recovering. So if you're not sleeping, you're not recovering. And if you're going to break your body down a lot, you better find ways to build it back up. And the only way to do that is get a lot of sleep.
–Tom Brady, American Football Player

Listen, leaders have to bring *energy* to the table. Energy creates momentum. When you have momentum, you look better. When you don't have momentum, you look worse than you really are. If you want to live a wealthy life, you have to properly manage your energy.

CHAPTER 7

RELATIONAL WEALTH CONFIDENCE

THE RELATIONSHIPS AND CONNECTIONS NECESSARY TO CREATE AND OPEN MORE DOORS

I F YOU'RE ANYTHING LIKE ME, I'm sure at some point in the course of your life you've heard someone utter the phrase, "There are no shortcuts to success." Do you personally believe that to be true? *Is* it true? For a great part of my life, I believed it as much as I believed the grass was green and the sky was blue. Now I believe something a bit different.

There was a knock on my mother-in-law's door. It was an old friend of mine who stopped by to join us for dinner. He didn't show up empty-handed. He came to give me a gift he felt impressed to buy me. At the end of supper, he handed me a high-quality $29.99 magazine full of pictures of the most beautiful homes in the Tampa Bay Area.

I thanked him with a puzzled look and then he said, "Don't let your current negative circumstances convince you that this is the best it can get. You need to keep dreaming big! Take some time to look through this book and find the house of your dreams, rip out the picture, and put it on your refrigerator door. When you go to the refrigerator, look at the house and imagine yourself owning it, and then boldly say, "I will live in this house in my future!"

LIVING WEALTHY MINDSET

DON'T JUDGE PEOPLE ON WHAT YOU SEE ON THEIR OUTSIDE. MOST PEOPLE WHO HAVE MONEY TO HELP FUND YOUR DREAMS DON'T WEAR HIGH MILAN FASHION, DRIVE EXOTIC ITALIAN SPORTS CARS, OR FLASH LOUIS VUITTON ACCESSORIES. PRETENDERS PARADE THEIR MONEY **OUTSIDE**, BUT USUALLY DON'T HAVE MONEY **INSIDE** THEIR BANK ACCOUNT.

Honestly, I thought he was crazy. But the next morning, my wife and I sat at the table and thumbed through the magazine. We allowed our imaginations to run wild as we found our mini-mansion dream house together. We figured we could *maybe* afford to live in one like it when we turned about 60 years of age. But we followed his instructions and put the picture on our refrigerator and declared that one day we would live in a home like that.

A few months later we decided to take a drive to one of the most prestigious gated communities in our area. To our amazement, we found a house that looked a lot like our picture on the refrigerator. As we gazed with awe at the beautiful house, I noticed an old, faded FOR SALE sign hidden in the bushes.

Suddenly, confidence rose up in my heart as the words of Jesus came into my mind: "If you can believe, all things are possible to him who believes" (Mark 9:23). With confidence, I picked up my phone and called the number, acting like I had all the money in the world to buy it. I scheduled an appointment for us to see the house and agreed on a price to buy the house with the owner that day. We had only one challenge to overcome—WE DIDN'T HAVE ANY MONEY.

I had one month to get the money. I thought I needed a financial miracle—like out of the blue receiving a check in the mail. I went to the mailbox every day, but received nothing but stacks of junk mail.

One afternoon, with only 3 days left until closing, a strange call came to my office. "There's a guy who wants to have breakfast with you." I actually remembered who this guy was. He always wore one of his *free* "I gave blood" T-shirts and baggy faded shorts, and drove around in an ugly, beat-up Toyota Corolla. When I prayed for open doors, I never imagined it would come packaged like this.

To my surprise, while eating biscuits and gravy, I learned that he lived in the same gated neighborhood where we wanted to live. I told him I was going to buy a house down the street from him, but needed financing. He chuckled and said, "I've been known to loan money to people to buy houses. Pick out your house and I'll loan you the money for it."

Wait! What!? I about fell off my chair. "Seriously? I'm supposed to close in the next few days." He simply replied, "Just tell me how much the house is and I'll have my attorney draw up the paperwork."

"Do you want to check my credit report or see my income from my taxes?"

"No, I've watched you over the years and know you're a man of character."

The money transferred into our account one day before closing, and one month later, my wife and I moved into our dream home. Yes! What we thought would take us years happened in a matter of months.

Law of Acceleration: When you decide what you want and start moving toward your desired outcome, your desired outcome starts moving toward you at a rapid rate.

God opened two relationship doors to help me radically and quickly change my living arrangements and increase my wealth. One coached me at the dinner table to dream big, and the other one, while at a breakfast table, financed my dream.

LIVING WEALTHY MINDSET

THERE IS A SHORTCUT TO LIVING WEALTHY AND ACHIEVING SUCCESS—RELATIONSHIPS!

I now believe that the *quality* of our relationship network determines the *quantity* of our influence and impact on a wide variety of people.

I was teaching on this subject at a seminar when a young, struggling couple came up to me. "Getting wealthy is just all about who you know," he said, dripping with sarcasm. I replied, "Yes! And the quicker you understand that fact, the faster your life will change. Don't be angry that relationship wealth is so valuable to your success in life; just start becoming the person you need to be so you can attract divine connections in your life." They walked away with a better understanding and a clear path toward relationship wealth success.

LIVING WEALTHY MINDSET

WHEN GOD WANTS TO BLESS YOU, HE BRINGS THE RIGHT PERSON INTO YOUR LIFE. WHEN THE ENEMY WANTS TO DESTROY YOU, HE BRINGS THE WRONG PERSON INTO YOUR LIFE. IT TAKES DISCERNMENT TO DETERMINE THE DIFFERENCE!

AN ACCELERATED BOOK DEAL

Another dream of mine was for my writings to penetrate the secular marketplace. I knew I needed a large, secular New York publisher to accept my manuscript if I was going to make an impact on a broader audience. But without having celebrity status or a well-known name, attracting a reputable and successful publisher takes a miracle.

At a conference I was attending I overcame my fears and reached out and invited to dinner a famous, one-million-plus, best-selling author. Hint: If you're going to invite a successful person to dinner, don't take them to McDonald's or the Golden Corral. Do it right. It's an investment, not just a meal.

My confidence was contagious, and without knowing me, he agreed to join me for dinner. While we developed a relationship at the dinner table, he listened as I explained my desire, my dream, of having my writings reach a larger audience, and he connected me that very night with a New York agent who helped me land an advance (money paid up-front to publish my book before it was even finished!) with Penguin Publishers (the second-largest secular publisher in the world). A miracle—over the dinner table!

LIVING WEALTHY MINDSET

I ALWAYS PAY FOR DINNER WHEN WITH HIGHLY SUCCESSFUL LEADERS. PAY ANY PRICE TO BE IN THE PRESENCE OF GREATNESS. WHEN THEY KNOW YOU ALWAYS PAY, INVITATIONS WILL INCREASE. A $100 DINNER IS BETTER THAN A $10,000 COACHING BILL.

My next big dream was to speak at the largest business seminar company in the world. This dream was accomplished through a relationship with a pastor of a small church in my local area. Again, at a dinner table, he connected me with the CEO of that company. It was during lunch at one of my favorite beachfront restaurants that the CEO and I forged a friendship and he asked me to join the tour.

In the last year, through this seminar company alone, the CEO told me I spoke to more than 100,000 entrepreneurs and business leaders. I learned a significant lesson. Don't judge by size, because small hinges can swing open big doors.

You may be thinking, *Okay, Dr. J, I get it. You've had some incredible things happen to you through your relationships. But what makes you think that can happen to me?* My answer? I think it's time for you to discover the **Five Steps to Building Your Relational Wealth.**

STEP 1: ESTABLISH YOUR TABLE

Families gather together around our tables to eat special meals during the holiday seasons and birthdays. We take our spouse to a special restaurant for a romantic dinner. Sometimes we invite friends over for BBQ cookouts and sit together at picnic tables. Have you ever noticed that we develop quality conversations with one another around the table?

You have to create a table of people to surround you with support. There are people in your inner circle with whom you have given the privilege to break bread. They have your ear, so they can influence your mind, behavior, and ultimately your life direction.

You can only handle a certain number of relationships effectively. Once the table is full, nobody else can join you. So, you must establish your table with deliberate choices—every so often reflect if those at your table are positive or negative influences. Continually reach out to build a better table of companions.

STEP 2: EVALUATE YOUR TABLE

The year I spent living in my mother-in-law's house forced me to evaluate all my relationships. I had to ask myself the tough question: *Who's sitting at my table?*

As I evaluated the relationships in my life, I started to realize that my Relational Wealth was in the gutter. I had family and friends from my past who didn't want to grow, who didn't support my growth, and who were hurting me instead of helping me. Why were they still in my inner circle seated at my table?

Have you ever been in a room with an obnoxious odor—but after a while you don't notice it? This can happen with the people you choose to seat at your table. After a while, you start thinking like them and developing their habits, both good and bad.

LIVING WEALTHY MINDSET

INFLUENCE IS POWERFUL, YET SUBTLE. IF YOU HANG OUT AT A GARBAGE HEAP, YOU WILL SLOWLY BEGIN TO SMELL LIKE GARBAGE, AND NOT EVEN KNOW IT.

We must evaluate who we allow at the table of our inner circle. It can be difficult to weed out the undesirables, but it's mandatory. Let me coach you through this process. The following are the questions I asked myself during this process.

RELATIONAL WEALTH EVALUATION QUESTIONS:

- What type of people are sitting at my table?
- Where are they going in life?
- Are they successful?
- What are they doing for me?
- Are we challenging each other to grow or stay the same?
- What kind of books are they inspiring me to read, if any?
- Do they have the wisdom needed to help me achieve my assignment?
- What does their financial blueprint look like?

STEP 3: UPGRADE YOUR TABLE

I wanted to be a best-selling author, but I didn't know very many authors, much less best-selling authors. I wanted to be a millionaire, but didn't have any friends making seven figures. I wanted to be an internationally known leadership coach, but I didn't have a successful leadership coach myself.

None of the people I had in my life had achieved what I wanted for my future. Therefore, they couldn't help me go where I wanted to go in life. In order for me to change my life, I had to disconnect from *wrong* relationships in order to connect with the *right* relationships God had for me.

LIVING WEALTHY MINDSET

AS IN AN ELEVATOR, SOMETIMES ON YOUR WAY TO THE TOP, YOU HAVE TO STOP AND LET PEOPLE OFF TO GET TO THE NEXT LEVEL.

One wrong relationship can kill your momentum. All you need is one Jonah on your boat and the negative storms can start crashing down on you (Jonah 1:4). The men on the boat were innocent, but they mistakenly allowed Jonah to catch a ride. The only thing you can do when Jonah is on your boat is kick him off. Then the storms will stop (Jonah 1:15).

The Law of Replacement: When you lose one person from your life or team, you will attract someone even better if you wait patiently and pursue someone with more wisdom, skills, and talents. Until there is release, there cannot be increase.

This is where your confidence will be tested. Trust me! It's not easy to leave the relationships sitting at your table right now. It takes confidence to let go and reach for something new, bigger, and better.

LIVING WEALTHY MINDSET

TALK TO LIVING WEALTHY PEOPLE THROUGHOUT YOUR DAY. THEIR ENERGY, EXCITEMENT, POSITIVE ATTITUDE, AND INNER STRENGTH IS SO INSPIRING THAT YOU WILL FIND YOURSELF FEELING MORE EMPOWERED JUST BY LISTENING TO THEM.

You see, longtime relationships make you feel safe and secure. They don't challenge you. They don't require you to think differently. They simply accept you for who you are because they are on the same level as you or even below you and look up to you. You think they're your friends, but they are really the enemy of your potential.

My BEST friend is the one who brings out the BEST in me.
–Henry Ford

STEP 4: CREATE A NEW TABLE

Create a new, confident, and competent table of Living Wealthy people. Now is the time to start building your new table with those who can really help you. Who do you want at your table? Moral, successful, wealthy, and confident people who really believe in you and your vision for the future.

Choose friendships that build, support, and reinforce your character, competence, and confidence for Living Wealthy. Be very selective.

There will always be two types of people in your life: confidence shakers or confidence makers. Confidence shakers love to release words that discourage you. They always see something negative in what you are trying to accomplish.

Competence: The ability to do something.

Confidence: Your belief about your competence.

It's going to take **confidence** to connect with more competent, higher-level, wealthier, and successful people.

If you want to improve your golf, tennis, or basketball game, you must play with someone who is better than you. Running with the best will cause you to better your best. Yes, it can be intimidating and uncomfortable at first, but it is a major key to increasing both your competence and your confidence.

FAMILY TIES

Who is the wealthiest and most successful person in your family? My grandfather ran a very successful insulation company in our city. Only one problem—everybody in the family hated him. Why? Because he had money and he wouldn't give it to them to bail them out of all their stupidity. I fell into the trap of being envious of my grandfather's success instead of learning from him. Sadly, I kept my distance.

I have never had a hater who is doing better than me.
–Bishop T.D. Jakes

The greatest gift anyone can give you is access. I could have had open access to my grandfather. When successful people give you their time, don't take it lightly. And by all means give them as much of your time as possible. If they do give you access, don't forget to thank them. When a person is grateful for my time, I reward them with more of it.

STEP 5: ASSIGN PRIMARY SEATS AT YOUR TABLE

When thinking of the people we want seated at our table, we can learn a great deal from Joseph's rags-to-riches story in the Bible. It is filled with many different relationships, both helpful and hurtful.

Joseph had a measure of God's favor on his life. At a young age he was given divine dreams and visions concerning his future success (Genesis 37). Along the way, though, it seemed his brothers had derailed his destiny. But not so—he stood firm on his beliefs and the end of his story is one of success.

LIVING WEALTHY MINDSET

MONEY ISN'T A MIRACLE NOR A MYSTERY. MONEY IS SIMPLY THE REWARD FOR SOLVING PROBLEMS AND MEETING PEOPLE'S NEEDS. THE SIZE OF THE PROBLEM DETERMINES THE SIZE OF THE REWARD. HAVE CONFIDENCE TO PRAY FOR BIG PROBLEMS TO SOLVE.

Some think Joseph's greatest skill was his ability to interpret dreams. But I see Joseph's greatest skill as his ability to solve big problems. Joseph helped seven people solve their problems, which gained him influence and wealth (Genesis 39–41).

Joseph helped:

1. Potiphar – Joseph caused Potiphar's house and fields to prosper

2. Prison warden – Joseph was put in charge and the prison prospered

3. Butler – Joseph interpreted his dream

4. Baker – Joseph interpreted his dream

5. Pharaoh – Joseph interpreted his dream

6. Family – Joseph saved his family from economic disaster and famine

7. Egypt – Joseph saved the entire nation from famine

There are two kinds of people on earth: 1) Problem-solvers and 2) Problems. Where there is a problem, there is an opportunity for wealth, success, and significance. On your road to achieving your dream, you have to help others solve their problems.

Joseph's journey from the pit to the palace required three different influential connections to help him solve his wealth problems. The baker, the butler, and Pharaoh.

Bakers are those who have the recipe and pull all the ingredients together to achieve their desired results. Oftentimes, we have the raw goods to achieve our assignment, but we haven't acquired the art of putting them all together. Raw talent is great, but no one wants to eat a handful of flour, yeast, and water. Yuck! Yet, when those ingredients are properly mixed and baked, we all enjoy a freshly baked piece of bread. That's the baker's job. The baker brings all the ingredients necessary to help you manifest your dreams.

A butler is someone who can open new doors for you. One night, after I had dined at an extravagant restaurant, the valet approached and asked me for the ticket to retrieve my Mercedes. A moment later the valet arrived in a gorgeous Rolls-Royce Wraith. He hopped out of the car and said, "Here you are, Dr. Johnson, your vehicle." I thought, *Hallelujah, the butler hath opened unto me a new door!* We had a good laugh about the mix-up.

LIVING WEALTHY MINDSET

PEOPLE ARE LIKE DOORS HELPING YOU MOVE THROUGH ONE SEASON TO ANOTHER, ONE LEVEL TO ANOTHER, AND ONE RELATIONSHIP TO ANOTHER.

The butler is a connecter who can lead you to a door of brand-new, amazing relationships. Make sure you have a butler seated at your table.

It was obvious to those around Joseph that he was destined for the throne. But without a king seated at his table, it would be impossible for Joseph to achieve his dream. It was through a series of unfortunate circumstances that Joseph was brought face to face with Pharaoh.

Later, Joseph describes the series of events to his brothers this way: "You intended to harm me, but God intended it for good to accomplish what is now being done, the saving of many lives" (Genesis 50:20 NIV). Through Joseph's dream, an entire nation was spared many years of famine. Because of this, Pharaoh found himself seated at Joseph's table of destiny, and Joseph was promoted to a place of authority over Egypt.

Of all the people invited to sit at your table, make room for the baker, butler, and Pharaoh.

BIG, IMPORTANT QUESTIONS

Open your cell phone and look at your favorites list. Who do you see?

Of those currently on your favorites list and those seated at your table, which relationships can help you achieve your destiny?

Begin investing in those relationships now. Start today.

CHAPTER 8

PROFESSIONAL WEALTH CONFIDENCE

NOURISHING YOUR POTENTIAL WITH EDUCATION, EMPOWERMENT, AND EXPERIENCE

OFTEN IN OUR QUEST TOWARD SPIRITUAL GROWTH, we can find ourselves unintentionally devaluing the importance of our work lives. Many people have a "One of these days I'm going to tell my boss to take this job and shove it" attitude toward our work. This is truly a desperate situation. In fact, 87 percent of people admit to hating their jobs.

Here's the real tragedy. The majority of us spend nearly 2,080 hours a year here on earth functioning professionally in the marketplace. If you hate your work, you're dead 30-40 years before it's official.

Your work was designed by God to help you discover your God-given potential and to pull that potential out of you. Without work, you cannot discover your true gifts, talents, and skills or what you could be, do, achieve, or have in this life.

Moreover, when God gives someone wealth and possessions, and the ability to enjoy them, to accept their lot and be happy in their toil—this is a gift of God (Ecclesiastes 5:19 NIV).

Your profession, your work, is a gift from God. It's also the vehicle God has ordained to bring the joy of achievement, riches, and wealth into your life. There can be no greatness without work.

God is a worker. God labored six days to birth the heavens, the earth, the universe. What is God still doing? Working! Jesus acknowledges the importance of work. He said, "My Father is always at his work to this very day, and I too am working" (John 5:17 NIV).

When people say, "Look, even God took time off from work," I like to jokingly respond, "Well, when you create the entire universe out of thin air in less than a week, then we can talk about a weekend off for you."

Some have said that work was the result of "sin." Nothing could be further from the truth. Before the fall, God gave Adam the gift of work and instructed him to do five things to discover his full potential. Let's count them:

1. Exercise rulership over the earth and subdue it.
2. Plant seeds.
3. Tend, guard, and keep the garden.
4. Care for Eve.
5. Name all the animals.

He also gave the command to both Adam and Eve to be fruitful and multiply. Why? Because God loves and rewards our work.

The one who plants and the one who waters have one purpose, and they will each be rewarded according to their own labor. For we are co-workers in God's service; you are God's field, God's building (1 Corinthians 3:8-9 NIV).

Throughout the remainder of this chapter, you will learn how to experience increase in your professional life in a way that honors God and inspires others—for your good and God's glory.

Let's commit to going after it together.

THREE STRATEGIES TO MAXIMIZING YOUR PROFESSIONAL WEALTH POTENTIAL

STRATEGY 1: FULLY EMBRACE YOUR PROFESSION AS A SPIRITUAL ACTIVITY

The first thing to understand is that your career, job, profession, or business is a spiritual activity. Wherever God's people gather, you will find the church. Whether people are gathered in a cathedral or a cubicle, you will find the church in action.

Where you find the church, you will also find God's ministers. Traditionally, we see ministers as pastors or employees of a particular church. Sure, God has the five-fold ministry to lead and equip the saints, but God has given every believer a ministry of impacting the world around them.

And this is from God, who reconciled us to himself through Christ and gave us the ministry of reconciliation: that God was reconciling the world to himself in Christ, not counting people's sins against them. And he has committed to us the message of reconciliation (2 Corinthians 5:18-19 NIV).

YOUR PROFESSION IS YOUR MINISTRY

When you start seeing your profession as a form of ministry, you will see your profession as the pulpit you preach from every day. Your sermon isn't the traditional three points and an altar call. It's the transformational story of how God provides opportunities every day to move people from where they are to where they want to be—in the workplace, at home, and in every aspect of life.

It's your rags-to-riches story, or your testimony, that will destroy and demolish wrong belief systems others have about God and success. Your powerful testimony will be a tool to crush the limiting lies of other people's stories about why they can't achieve big things or Live Wealthy.

LIVING WEALTHY MINDSET

YOUR PERSONAL SUCCESS PREACHES TO OTHERS WITHOUT SAYING A WORD.

It's important for pastors and Christian leaders to grow people spiritually. However, we need a balanced approach. We must not forget to empower believers professionally as well. Failure to do so causes us to have highly spiritual church members, who are amateurs in their professions. Do the math. Eventually, we end up with a financially broke church with very little influence in the world.

LIVING WEALTHY MINDSET

LACK OF FINANCIAL RESOURCES FOR THE LOCAL CHURCH INDICATES A LACK OF MARKETPLACE EQUIPPING.

Don't be afraid of the marketplace—integrate and dominate your space! During my professional crisis, I wanted to shrink back and isolate myself from everybody. It's the most natural response for most humans in tough times. However, marketplace transformation comes from integration, not isolation. Remember, we are to be the salt of the world.

Many spiritual people have been taught to divide their lives into two categories: spiritual and secular. So everything done on Sunday is incredible and awesome. But, Monday through Friday when it's time to go to work, it's back to the drudge or back to the bad, evil world.

Especially in biblical times, Jews saw the world, as created by God, both as physical and spiritual with no division. When they read the Torah and prayed, they were being spiritual. When they did business in the workplace and made money, they were being spiritual. Perhaps this is why the same Hebrew root word *avad* is used to describe a person who is worshiping Yahweh as well as a person who is at work serving customers. Think of it: the same word used for worship is the same word used for work.

Jews viewed success as a moral and spiritual obligation and responsibility—we should too. Sadly, the Greek philosophy of duality, the separation between physical and spiritual, slowly replaced the Jewish influence as the hooks of the Roman Empire began to ensnare the church.

We know the professions of many men and women in the New Testament church, because they saw this was an important part of their spiritual lives. Joseph and Jesus were carpenters. Matthew was a tax collector. Peter and Andrew were commercial fishermen. Luke was a doctor. Lydia was a sales professional. Paul, Aquila, and Priscilla were tentmakers.

Change how you think and feel about your profession and watch how successful you will become as your influence naturally increases.

STRATEGY 2: DISCOVER THE DIAMOND WITHIN

You don't need to look very far for wealth and prosperity. One of your greatest wealth-creating tools is actually so close to you, so obvious, but you haven't seen it. What is it?

In his classic book *Acres of Diamonds*, Russell Conwell, founder of Temple University, tells a story about an African farmer, who, bent on hunting for diamonds, sells his farm to journey off to find riches. After coming up short, he gets word a few weeks later that the new owner of the farm had discovered acres of diamonds on the property he had sold.

The problem was for him and is for us—diamonds look just like chunks of rocks. They need to be cut and polished to bring out their true beauty and value. Likewise in your life, there are diamonds—strengths, gifts, and abilities—under your own feet, but they may be unrealized, disguised as hard work or something else entirely.

LIVING WEALTHY MINDSET

IDENTIFYING AND MAXIMIZING YOUR GREATEST STRENGTH IS THE KEY TO FUNCTIONING IN YOUR PURPOSE, IGNITING YOUR PASSION, AND LIVING WEALTHY.

Have you discovered the diamond within? Your profession, career, or business is really your ability to take your greatest strength and use it to add value to others. It's about finding the gift you have been divinely given by God and giving it away to the world.

LIVING WEALTHY MINDSET

FINDING YOUR GIFT, GROWING YOUR GIFT, AND GIVING YOUR GIFT AWAY IS THE SECRET TO LIVING WEALTHY.

Money follows mastery. Pick one thing you do well and master it! Money is a sign that you are doing what you are created to do. Also, the lack of money is a sign you haven't discovered and developed your diamond within. You are an amateur, not a master.

To grow you, you must know you. The following is a way you can start narrowing your ideal profession down to one you can pursue. Every profession can be broken down into *three diamond categories:*

1. *Hands Professional* - Mechanics, Dentists, Carpenters, etc.

2. *Head Professional* - Engineers, Web Developers, Teachers, etc.

3. *Mouth Professional* - Sales Professionals, Paid Speakers, Defense Attorneys, etc.

Stop and ask yourself, *Am I a hands, head, or mouth person?* Think about the careers that complement that particular strength of yours. Consider the steps you need to take to pursue that career. Then take action!

LIVING WEALTHY MINDSET

SUCCESS HAPPENS WHEN YOUR PROFESSION, PURPOSE, AND POWER GIFTS CONVERGE.

When you discover your greatest strength, concentrate all your focus and energy into maximizing that wealth treasure given to you by God. Trust me, your gift will make room for you in this world, and financial rewards and influence will naturally follow.

92

COACHING QUESTIONS

What is something I can easily do, but is hard for everyone else?

What do others say I am really great at?

STRATEGY 3: BECOME THE 10X EXPERT

When I coach my clients, I always challenge and stretch them to set a goal to become ten times better at what they do. Most want their business to get 10X bigger. But I've found that if you focus your efforts on getting 10X *better* at your craft, the world will demand that you get 10X *bigger*.

Daniel is one of my favorite characters in the Bible. He was a highly educated man who was schooled in both the Hebrew and Babylonian colleges of his day. The following is what the king said about Daniel:

> And in all matters of wisdom and understanding about which the king examined them, he found them **ten times better** than all the magicians and astrologers who were in all his realm (Daniel 1:20).

Daniel was a marketplace man of God who became 10X better than the secular leaders of his day. He was eventually promoted to a top political position. So what was Daniel's key to success, wealth, and influence? Excellence!

> Then this Daniel distinguished himself above the governors and satraps, because an **excellent spirit** was in him; and the king gave thought to setting him over the whole realm (Daniel 6:3).

LIVING WEALTHY MINDSET

INVEST IN YOUR MOST VALUABLE ASSET—
YOU!

All the confidence in the world is meaningless if you don't have the knowledge it takes to put your confidence to use. Confidence is built on what you know.

Ignorance breeds fear. The more you learn about your subject, the less power fear has over you. When we have limited information, our doubts dominate us.

If we value excellence and are passionately pursuing improvement, our confidence and competence grow, and we become experts in our craft. How do you gauge if you are truly an expert? When people come to you for answers, and you have the answers—then you know you are an expert in your field. So how do you get to that point? I can help take you there with the following **10X Expert Growth Strategy.**

An expert has special knowledge of a subject or special skill in a field of action. And becoming an expert is easy, if you have the right formula. I learned a simple formula that skyrocketed my income and I became an expert, which helped me become known as an internationally acclaimed confidence coach.

Expert Formula: $R + S + 5Y = 5\%$

Here are the formula details: Read (R) one hour a day about your subject (S) for 5 years (Y) and you will rise to the top 5 percent in your field.

Do you want to increase your income? If so, remember, the market will pay an expert wage for an expert. If you don't like your income, you can do something about it by becoming an expert.

LIVING WEALTHY MINDSET

SOMETHING YOU DON'T HAVE IS BECAUSE OF SOMETHING YOU DON'T KNOW.

How did Dr. Martin Luther King Jr. so quickly gain respect and admiration as a leader? He was both confident and competent. Martin Luther King Jr. was prepared to lead because he had gained a first-rate education—both in terms of formal schooling and informal mentoring. He had both book smarts and practical wisdom.

King enrolled at Morehouse College in Atlanta when he was 15 years of age, and he earned a bachelor's degree in sociology. He went on to graduate from Crozer Theological Seminary with a Bachelor of Divinity, and then completed his Ph.D. in systematic theology at Boston University.

Another inspirational figure is Ben Carson, MD. Dr. Carson's incredible life story is told in his memoir and movie, *Gifted Hands.* He says the following about his personal experience:

It doesn't matter if you come from the inner city. People who fail in life are people who find lots of excuses. It's never too late for a person to recognize that they have potential in themselves.

After a pretty rough start as a nearly illiterate child, raised by a single mother in the inner city of Detroit, Carson graduated from Yale University. He then went on to become the first neurosurgeon to successfully separate conjoined twins joined at the head. He is also the youngest director of pediatric surgery in the history of Johns Hopkins Hospital.

LIVING WEALTHY MINDSET

PREPARATION TODAY ASSURES CONFIDENCE TOMORROW.

The quality of your preparation determines the level of your confidence. The level of your confidence determines the quality of your performance. What you are doing today is preparing you for tomorrow. When you learn to do the right things daily, you are guaranteed success in your tomorrow. If you continue to do the wrong things today, you are guaranteed failure in your future.

I prepare myself until I know I can do what I have to do.
–Joe Namath

The preparation period can be tedious. It takes a lot of work to prepare, which is why so few people do it. However, preparation today gives you confidence for tomorrow. Therefore, preparation today brings success in your future. You can claim to be surprised once; after that you're unprepared.

Choose to be one of the most successful people you know, and choose it again and again every hour of every day for the rest of your life.

Your talent may be enormous. Your potential may be great. But talent and potential unannounced to the rest of the world is wasted, and it's going to take financial wealth to let the world know you exist. You will learn how to experience financial wealth in the next chapter.

CHAPTER 9

FINANCIAL WEALTH CONFIDENCE

MONEY CAN'T SAVE YOU, BUT IT CAN MAKE YOU HAPPY

WAIT, WHAT IS THE NAME OF THIS CHAPTER? Don't worry about it right now. Just keep reading. It's now time to really deal with the elephant in the room. Perhaps you've done everything the prosperity preachers said to do, but you're still not rich. You have attended all the seminars. You've listened to the biblically inspirational messages by the current popular pastor. You have prayed, confessed, declared, and given sacrificially in the offering bucket. And nothing.

Now you're asking yourself, *Why haven't I been able to turn my dream into reality?* The answer is always the same, my friend. Love it or hate it, you need money to fulfill your God-given destiny.

What is your attitude about money? Positive or negative? I had to learn the hard way that money tends to flow toward people who are positive about it and away from people who have a negative attitude.

Your relationship with money is like your relationship with people. I used to arrogantly say, "Money's not important." Well, what if I told my wife she wasn't important to me? What do you think she would do? You guessed it. She would be long gone. Of course I'm not equating money with my dear wife, but you can understand the concept. A healthy relationship with money attracts and allows for more of it to come to you.

LIVING WEALTHY MINDSET

WHAT YOU DON'T HONOR IN LIFE, YOU LOSE.
WHAT YOU DO HONOR IN LIFE, YOU GAIN.

What you set your affection on will set its affection on you. This is a spiritual principle. James 4:8 tells us that when you draw near to God, He draws near to you! Likewise, when you give attention to the spiritual, mental, physical, relational, professional, and financial parts of your life, the resources to improve each of these areas will show up.

Money is a tool you need to get things done. It's a fact that can't be ignored.

In 1943, in his book *Motivation and Personality,* Abraham Maslow introduced the world to an interesting theory. His thought was that human beings can't even begin to think about higher existential needs, such as self-actualization or growing to their full potential, if they don't have their basic needs fulfilled such as air, food, water, shelter, clothes, and a variety of other essential needs.

Money isn't the most important thing in life, but it's reasonably close to oxygen on the "gotta have it" scale.
–Zig Ziglar

Many pastors and leaders are banging their heads against the wall wondering why people who listen to their teachings remain stagnant, unable to experience growth. The answer is quite simple if you measure Maslow's theory against most people's financial condition. The majority are so financially broke that they can't entertain the thought or maintain the work it takes to grow into their maximum potential.

The following is a snapshot of the financial condition of most people today:

- 76% of people live paycheck to paycheck
- 47% don't have $500 in the bank for an emergency
- 43% of American households spend more money than they earn
- 65% said they are losing sleep because of money this year
- 41% have medical bill problems and are working to pay off debt
- 70% of all Americans believe that "debt is a necessity in their lives"
- 40 million Americans are paying off student loan debt
- 49 million people are living in poverty in the United States

I was raised in a home with absolutely no financial wealth intelligence at all. My parents worked in construction. They struggled their entire lives under the intense pressure of living paycheck to paycheck. They worked hard one week to complete a construction project. Got paid with cash. Then spent the weekends partying away all the money. The new week began with no money in their pockets, and once again they had to scrimp to get by until the next job was finished. Then the cycle started all over again. Rinse and repeat.

When I was a child I dreaded winter because the snow would bring construction to a squelching halt. With my parents' short-term thinking, they never saved for the cold winters. Consequently, we would be flat broke for 3 or 4 months straight every year. Having the electric turned off at your house when it's twenty degrees below zero isn't fun.

Let's fast forward together.

THE MILLIONAIRE ROUNDTABLE

After I learned the strategies to turn my finances completely around, I was quite surprised and honored the day an interesting invitation came to my office. I was invited to deliver a keynote presentation at a book publisher's expo. What a confidence boosting thought it was to go from flunking kindergarten and barely being able to read in my early twenties to keynoting an authors' event!

After my speech, I was asked to participate in the millionaire roundtable Q&A with nine other successful authors. I remember the feeling of fulfillment as I walked on stage thinking of my childhood when I sat at our kitchen table eating government cheese and peanut butter sandwiches, to now sitting at a table with millionaires.

The first question the audience asked the roundtable participants was, "What was the beginning point of your rise to becoming a millionaire?" Each person at the table said the same thing, "The first thing I had to change was my mindset about wealth and money."

CREATING YOUR MILLIONAIRE MINDSET

It's time for a brain transplant. It's time to break down the barriers that are preventing your mind from embracing a healthy understanding about money. We are going to examine three foundational mindsets that you must have to start increasing your financial wealth intelligence and ultimately your bank account. Let's get started.

MINDSET 1: YOU MUST CONTINUALLY CHALLENGE AND CHANGE YOUR CURRENT BELIEF SYSTEMS ABOUT MONEY.

What got you here can't get you there. You cannot change your financial problems until you are willing to change your belief systems. To begin the journey of renewing your mind concerning financial wealth, you must come to the place where you realize that your belief systems are not completely accurate.

The great unifying summary statement of all religions and philosophies is this: *You become what you think about most.* Solomon was one of the richest and wisest men in history. His insight was, "For as he thinks in his heart, so is he" (Proverbs 23:7).

If you think of yourself as poor—you are poor. If you see yourself as a millionaire—you may be one. Your inner world ultimately becomes a reality of your outer world. How and what you think on the inside will manifest on the outside.

There are really only two types of belief systems: *empowering* and *unempowering.*

If you aren't where you want to be, somewhere hidden in your story is an *unempowering* belief system. It's a negative story created out of your imagination. Everyone has a story—an excuse why they can't succeed or become a Kingdom millionaire. Here's the thing, though. You can make excuses or you can make money, but you can't make both.

LIVING WEALTHY MINDSET

MONEY HAS NO FEELINGS AND DOESN'T CARE ABOUT YOUR STORY, YOUR GEOGRAPHY, YOUR GENDER, OR YOUR RACE. IT COMES TO ANYONE WHO ATTRACTS IT.

When you start thinking about your story, remember, there have been people throughout history in the same situation as you are in right now, if not worse, who have achieved incredible things despite not having resources in the beginning. However, they didn't let their current financial state stop them from dreaming big and taking massive action. They defied the odds and figured out a way to get the resources needed to fulfill their dreams.

LIVING WEALTHY MINDSET

YOUR VISION SHOULD ALWAYS BE BIGGER THAN YOUR CHECKBOOK. THE SIZE OF YOUR VISION DETERMINES THE SIZE OF YOUR PROVISION.

I still remember the pain I felt of being flat broke as I scraped through the ashtray of my car to dig up enough change to buy a breakfast burrito at McDonald's. (In Chapter 1, I was desperate to find change for a taco. Times were tough!) Depression set in as I drove home. I saw a homeless man on the side of the road with a "Will work for food" sign and thought, *That'll be me tomorrow!*

Things got worse after I returned home, walked into my office, and saw a huge stack of maxed-out credit card bills on my desk, next to the negative balance in my checkbook. I spent the next few hours mentally and verbally abusing myself, *I'm so stupid. I'm never going to get out of this mess. What a loser.*

When the opportunity came the next day to move into my mother-in-law's house, it was the saving grace we needed to keep us from being homeless or living out of my car. A car, by the way, that I owed more on than it was worth. This was the toughest time of my life, yet it was the best time of my life. Why? Because often what we call a crisis, God calls a classroom.

It was in this classroom where I began the process of transforming my mindset about what I believed about money and rebuilding my confidence to get it.

I experienced several drastic changes in my belief systems concerning financial wealth—from one side of the paradigm to the other—in the first decade of my faith journey. I went from believing poverty was the pathway for spirituality, to believing God wanted me to be radically rich. Then, for a season, I bought into the philosophy that money and finances weren't important. It's all about my spirituality. Yet this mindset left me with too many unanswered questions.

LIVING WEALTHY MINDSET

A MIND FILLED WITH UNANSWERED QUESTIONS IS A MIND FULL OF DOUBT— CAUSING STAGNATION. A MIND FULL OF SOLUTIONS IS A MIND FULL OF CONFIDENCE.

In my utter frustration, I chose to turn off the television preachers and read through the entire Bible myself—from Genesis to Revelation—to find out what God's Word really had to say about financial wealth. I examined the Bible in its totality, not just picking one or two Scriptures out of context and establishing an entire belief system on it, like I had seen so many others do.

What I learned comes down to three questions that changed my mindset dramatically for the better. I meditated on these questions and then used my spiritual confidence to cast down wrong ideas about God and wealth. I call these **Reality Check Questions.**

If God is ashamed of wealth:

- Why does He have so much of it? (Psalm 50:7-12)
- Why did He give us word pictures in the Bible about the opulence of Heaven? (Revelation 21:18-21)
- Why would an extravagantly wealthy God want His children to be poor? (Matthew 7:8-12)

Now, in the movie theater of your mind, begin to answer these questions for yourself.

Mindset 2: You must be absolutely convinced that it's God's will to make you financially wealthy.

Let me assure you that you can have confidence for living financially wealthy because God has actually already promised this to you when He made a covenant with your father of faith, Abraham. God says to Abraham in Genesis 12:2-3 (NIV):

I will make you into a great nation, and I will bless you; I will make your name great, and you will be a blessing. I will bless those who bless you, and whoever curses you I will curse; and all peoples on earth will be blessed through you.

What did this promise of blessing produce in Abraham's life? Abraham became abundantly wealthy in all six areas of his Wealth Quotient:

- **Spiritually** - His faith in God was strong (Romans 4:20)
- **Mentally** - He was mentally convinced that his promise from God would happen (Roman 4:21)
- **Physically** - His health was good; he lived until he was 175 years old
- **Relationally** - His entire family highly honored and respected him
- **Professionally** - He was a successful expert as a herdsman

- **Financially** - He had an abundance of financial wealth in silver, gold, flocks, herds, camels, donkeys, and real estate (Genesis 24:34-35)

This wealth agreement empowered Abraham to be financially prosperous himself so he could ultimately serve others. God's desire wasn't that just one man would become wealthy and help others; it was His desire that "all peoples on the earth will be blessed." Hey! That means you!

This is why the Jewish community controls 80 percent of the financial wealth in the world. They expect to become financially wealthy because they understand it's first and foremost part of their spiritual heritage from their father, Abraham.

Ready for some great news? When you believe in Jesus Christ, you are adopted into the family of God as Abraham's son or daughter. This means that you qualify for the same covenant wealth of Abraham, Isaac, Jacob, and Joseph. The following is New Testament proof that Abraham's covenant wealth belongs to you as a believer:

Understand, then, that those who have faith are children of Abraham. Scripture foresaw that God would justify the Gentiles by faith, and announced the gospel in advance to Abraham: "All nations will be blessed through you." So those who rely on faith are blessed along with Abraham, the man of faith (Galatians 3:7-9 NIV).

Today you can have confidence because the blessing of Abraham and the right to Living Wealthy has come to you through Jesus Christ. This is God's unchanging covenant with His unchanging purpose, which is to be a blessing to His human family on earth.

A loving and good Father doesn't want His children living in poverty and lack. God revealed His heart to lift people out of poverty and up in economic status when He says in Deuteronomy 15:4 (NIV), "There need be no poor people among you, for in the land the Lord your God is giving you to possess as your inheritance, he will richly bless you."

IS MONEY THE ROOT OF ALL EVIL?

Deeply ingrained into the philosophy of a post-early Christian religious culture dwells a lie masked in a Scripture that has paralyzed many from living the abundant life. What is this unempowering belief system? "The love of money is the root of all kinds of evil" (1 Timothy 6:10).

What if the meaning of this Scripture is actually the opposite of what many have been taught? Have you ever considered that the *lack* of money is the root of all evil?

Think about it:

- Lack of money causes thieves to break into houses and steal electronics and jewelry.
- Lack of money causes a drug lord to kill his distributor.
- Lack of money causes a woman to sell her body in prostitution.
- Lack of money causes a parent to sell a child into slavery.
- Lack of money causes a husband and wife to fight and eventually divorce.
- Lack of money causes people to be slaves at jobs they hate.
- Lack of money causes people to rip off other people.
- Lack of money causes businesses to shut the doors.
- Lack of money prevents people from receiving proper medical treatment.
- Lack of money is the number one cause of stress, and stress is the number one cause of heart attacks.
- Lack of money keeps a church from spreading the message of the Gospel, from buying property to build churches, and from paying pastors the salary needed and deserved.

Now that's what I call EVIL!

Let's take this a bit further.

Jesus says in Matthew 6:24 (NKJV), "You cannot serve both God and mammon." Mammon was known in Jewish culture in those days as an evil demonic spirit (not money or wealth itself) that people allowed to control them, manifesting in selfishness, covetousness, greed, and envy. The spirit of mammon says, "Make *me* the focus of your worship."

These were the people in His day who served mammon by leaving God out of their financial affairs. What does the spirit of mammon do?

1. It pressures you to make decisions for your life and destiny based solely on money.
2. It causes you to make consumer-driven purchases so you can keep up with the Joneses.

3. It tells preachers not to teach on wealth or money.

4. It causes you to hoard for yourself instead of becoming a blessing to others.

5. It wants to become an idol in your life so you no longer put the Kingdom first.

6. It wants you to continue in a slave mentality so you can't be financially free.

Many could read this and say, "But Scripture tells us we can't serve two masters!" True. I'm not suggesting you should serve two masters. I'm telling you to *become a master of money*. You either master money or money will master you. As long as you live a poor to middle-class life, money will always have the upper hand.

LIVING WEALTHY MINDSET

MONEY IS A POSITIVE GIFT YOU RECEIVE WHEN YOU SOLVE A PROBLEM OR MEET OTHERS' NEEDS.

CAN MONEY MAKE YOU HAPPY?

A word of caution: When you talk about money with middle class and poor people, most will quickly say, "Money doesn't make you happy." To find out if money makes you happy, don't consult the middle class. Talk to somebody who is financially rich.

I always warn others not to go to a bald barber, not to eat food cooked by a skinny chef, not to take weight loss advice from an overweight person, and never *ever* take financial advice from a poor person.

Most financially rich people will tell you there was a time when they were broke and now they are rich. They know the feeling on both sides of the spectrum. I have found that 98 percent of really rich people will say that they are much happier being rich than poor.

It's not just rich people from today who can confirm what I'm saying. The wealthy of Scripture agree with me as well:

A feast is made for laughter, wine makes life merry, and money is the answer for everything! (Ecclesiastes 10:19)

The blessing of the Lord makes one rich, and He adds no sorrow with it (Proverbs 10:22 NKJV).

When you hear, "Money won't make you happy," on the surface this cliché sounds good. However, you won't find one solid Bible verse that backs up this purely cultural statement. Let's consider:

1. If they have always been poor and never had any significant amount of money, how can they know if it can or it can't make people happy?

2. Most are just regurgitating what they have heard another person (who didn't have money) say, and it sounded like a good philosophy to repeat.

3. The poor usually haven't thought things through enough to realize that money creates feelings—good when you have it, and bad when you don't.

4. They haven't studied the new scientific studies that report how an increase of income increases happiness, especially for those earning less than $75,000 a year.

5. Most importantly, they may not be aware that Jesus said, "It is more blessed [and brings greater joy] to give than to receive" (Acts 20:35 AMP). Being able to contribute financial support to help others brings much happiness and joy.

Yes! Money makes me very happy when I watch our Destiny International college students walk across the stage at graduation and receive bachelor's, master's, or doctorate degrees, knowing that I donated the money to sponsor one of them.

Yes! Money makes me very happy when I take a struggling pastor to the mall and buy him or her new clothes or a nice pair of stylish shoes.

Yes! Money makes me very happy when I take my wife out on a date or to the mall and bless her with a new dress.

Yes! Money makes me very happy at Christmas time when I can help a poor, single mother and her children have a wonderful Christmas.

I think you get the point.

At the end of the day, even if money can't make you happy, I would rather be unhappy and rich, than unhappy and poor.

CHAPTER 10

UNLOCKING AND ACCESSING THE WEALTH VAULT

CHOOSING TO BE WILLING, WORTHY, AND CAPABLE OF BECOMING WEALTHY

ONE WEEK AFTER MY SPIRITUAL AWAKENING, God literally showed me a picture (revelation) of me speaking in a stadium to thousands and thousands of people. At that moment, my heart was saying, "Yes!" But then my head would say, "No! I could never do that."

I was at a very important crossroad where I had to make a life-changing decision. Was I going to accept the vision of the divine possibilities of who I could become, what I could have, and how I could help thousands of people? Or was I going to listen to my own lies, self-doubts, and unempowering belief systems about my own potential?

I believe you are at the same crossroad. I believe at the moment of decision, destiny is being shaped. Let me assure you, small decisions today go into your future and create HUGE outcomes tomorrow.

As my heart and mind battled for several days, I finally decided to go talk to a pastor. I told him my entire story. The drugs, the women, the alcohol—everything. Sadly, the pastor looked across the desk at me and said in a pious tone, "God doesn't use people like you. He only uses HOLY people to do the work of the ministry."

LIVING WEALTHY MINDSET

GOD WILL GIVE YOU A REVELATION THAT IS LARGER THAN YOUR SITUATION, SO YOU WILL HAVE THE MOTIVATION NECESSARY TO ARRIVE AT HIS DESTINATION FOR YOUR LIFE.

Thankfully, I didn't hit the delete button on the picture of my destiny. Rather, I listened to my confidence coach who said, "You are exactly the kind of person God uses to spread the good news!"

Sometimes your greatest destiny critics will come from well-meaning but religious people inside the church. And when it comes to the subject of money, trust me, you are floating in a small pool surrounded by dangerous sharks, snakes, and alligators who will try to kill your desire to become a Kingdom millionaire.

In the previous chapter, we looked at two of the three mindsets needed to become a Kingdom millionaire. In this chapter we are going to examine the third mindset. But before we move forward, ask yourself this question, *Does God really want me to be wealthy?*

You must come up with an answer to this question in your own head. It demands a YES or NO answer. You cannot have confidence for anything if you have unanswered questions in your head. As mentioned previously, unanswered questions produce doubt: "The one who doubts is like a wave of the sea, blown and tossed by the wind" (James 1:6 NIV).

The force and power of doubt lies in its ability to interrogate you with questions. Doubt is the prosecuting attorney who takes your confidence to live a financially wealthy lifestyle to court, trying to convince you that you will experience negative outcomes.

Doubt constantly asks:

- Can you really become wealthy? What if it's not for me?
- What if it will happen? What if it won't?
- Is it possible? What if it is impossible?
- Am I able to do this? What if I fail?
- What if my plan doesn't work out? What if it does?
- Do I deserve it? Am I good enough?
- Does God really want me to increase?
- Or does God just want me to be satisfied where I am?

The force of doubt is always with us. The "what ifs" and the "maybe, maybe nots" constantly try to turn our confidence to Living Wealthy into silly putty.

You need a level of confidence that is beyond just *positive thinking*. It's a *positive knowing* in your heart of hearts that God wants you to become financially wealthy. Confidence says, "I *know* without a shadow of doubt that God wants me to be a Kingdom millionaire."

LIVING WEALTHY MINDSET

THE VOICES OF DOUBT WILL ALWAYS SCREAM LOUDER THAN THE QUIET VOICE OF CONFIDENCE.

Again, this third mindset is a combination, not a key. If any of these aren't working together as a combo, you will remain stuck. The good news is, it's your decision to absorb all three into your life, therefore unlocking the doors to success.

Mindset 3: You must be *willing, worthy,* and *capable* of being financially wealthy.

God wanted the children of Israel to have the very best and promised to give them a land flowing with milk and honey. He promised them houses they didn't even build.

God sent twelve of His best leaders into the land to show them what their Living Wealthy future would look like. There was no question, uncertainty, or doubt—it was God's will and desire for them to Live Wealthy in the Promised Land.

WILLING

God believed they were worthy and capable of taking over the land. But they had to be *willing*. Isaiah 1:19 (NIV) says, "If you are **willing** and obedient, you shall eat the good of the land."

The problem was, ten of them didn't focus on the opportunity, but instead chose to focus on the challenge. They weren't *willing* to take the first step, and guess what? They never entered into the desired lifestyle that God wanted for them.

The leaders went in for 40 days to survey the land, and ten doubted the entire time. Consequently, they had to stay in the wilderness for 40 years.

LIVING WEALTHY MINDSET

YOUR DOUBT HAS DRAINED YOUR ACCOUNT. EVERY ONE DAY OF DOUBT EQUALS ONE YEAR WITHOUT!

Studies show that by the age of 45 you have already passed up the opportunity to be a millionaire two times.
–Johnny Wimbrey

Listen, the truth is this. We can debate the theology of wealth back and forth, but at the end of the day, it's your duty, obligation, and your moral responsibility to create wealth. If you say, "I'm content," or "I just need enough to cover my necessities and relax on Saturday," you're not fulfilling your destiny. If you're not willing to go after it with all you have, the Bible says you are a "wicked and lazy servant" (Matthew 25:26 NIV). Let's not forget the Parable of the Talents.

Whatever lot you have been handed in life, you have to be willing to be fruitful and multiply it. Bill Gates said it this way, "If you are born poor, it's not your mistake; but if you die poor, it is your mistake."

LIVING WEALTHY MINDSET

POVERTY IS A LOSING FORMULA. IT'S SO DARK AGES.

You think you're "good" financially? What about your children and your children's children? According to Proverbs 13:22 (NIV) a "good person leaves an inheritance for their children's children." Generational wealth. Not to mention loving your neighbor, offering a cloak if you have a spare, and not turning away anyone who comes to you with a need. You have to be *willing*. This is exactly what James meant when he said faith without works is dead. Choose right now in your mind to be a willing and financially wealthy servant.

WORTHY

Creating financial wealth is a worthy adventure. It is possible and available to everyone.

Don't devalue yourself and settle for the bare necessities. This is middle-class thinking. This is selfish living. Middle class is the great compromise. When you compromise your finances, you become unable to help others as God wants you to, because you are struggling to simply take care of yourself.

LIVING WEALTHY MINDSET

YOUR SELF-WORTH SETS THE TABLE FOR YOUR NET WORTH.

Although being in God's family is all the permission we need to succeed, we still feel unworthy because we see others who seem inherently *more* deserving of success. Yet no one is inherently more deserving of success than another. Others may do more to earn it. They may work harder at it. But no one begins more entitled to it than another. Being here on this planet is all the permission we need.

CAPABLE

There are two words that have crippled more dreams than any other: "I can't!" If you have spoken them often, then you probably realize by now how those words and that mindset has hurt you more than any external enemy.

The only limitations you have are those you set up in your own mind, or worse yet, permit others to set up for you by believing their lies.

Free your mind and your mouth from ever thinking or saying, "I can't," and you will be capable of achieving your God-given destiny.

LIVING WEALTHY MINDSET

GOD'S GREATEST PROBLEM ISN'T GETTING PEOPLE TO BELIEVE IN HIM—IT IS GETTING HIS PEOPLE TO BELIEVE IN THEMSELVES SO THEY CAN DO BIG THINGS FOR HIM.

God needs you to believe in your own abilities to increase each of the *six combinations* to Living Wealthy. This is the hard-core truth: if you don't believe in you, then God can't use you. God believed the children of Israel could live wealthy in the Promised Land, but they didn't believe in themselves (see Numbers 13:33). God couldn't use Gideon until he believed in himself (see Judges 6:15).

Joshua and Caleb had a confident "I CAN!" attitude, and they were the only two who lived the life God desired. Remember, the majority lack confidence in themselves and miss out on God's best for their lives. Dare to break away from the masses and believe in yourself. When God finds a man or woman who believes in themselves, the possibility for achievement is unlimited.

In a study of more than 500 successful men and women (most of whom started with nothing and eventually reached the top of their field), it was found that their one common belief was no matter what happened, they would ultimately be successful. They had unshakable confidence in their ability to overcome all difficulties and finally succeed. They looked upon every setback or disappointment as a learning experience that helped them to do more of the right things later on. Because of this belief, they eventually became unstoppable.[1]

If you want to receive the *rewards* the future holds in trust for you, then you must exercise the most important choice given to you by God as members of the human race by *maintaining total dominion over your thoughts and confidence level.*

Your confidence is an asset, a treasure of great value that must be protected accordingly. When you have a high confidence level, you can do the remarkable.

CONFIDENCE IS THE FUEL OF CHANGE!

When you recognize your personal power and unique gifts, you can make necessary changes to improve your life. If you don't like how something is going for you, change it. If you don't have enough money in the bank, change it. If something doesn't suit you, change it. If something doesn't please you, change it. You don't have to be the same after today. If you don't like your present address, change it—you're not a tree!

Maybe you still think, *Oh, I'm just an ordinary person. I just need to keep my normal, secure, comfortable job.* Well, if you are *just* a something, then you won't have to become *anything.*

Eliminating "just" and "I can't" words from your vocabulary and attitudes from your lives will eliminate the devastation of lack for good. Are other people breaking barriers and becoming wealthy? Of course. Anything one person can do, another can do. Go do it. Because *YOU can!*

BECOMING WEALTHY IS NO LONGER A CHOICE

Do you want to live an enjoyable lifestyle during retirement? If so, you need to be aware of the money you need—$100,000 a year at retirement, more or less, guarantees the freedom to enjoy life at that stage. At that figure per year, I have been told that at least $1.8 million needs to be invested early on in a person's career. Again, becoming a Kingdom millionaire is no longer an option. It's a must.

It's worse for a 42-year-old Gen Xer, whose $1 million at retirement will only generate an inflation-adjusted $19,000 a year when all is said and done. And a 32-year-old millennial planning to retire at 67 with 1 million would live below the poverty line. This is the new financial condition some will face called, "million-dollar poverty."

According to the Social Security Administration, if you observe any 100 people at the start of their working careers and follow them for 40 years until retirement age, here's what you'll find:

- Only 1 person will be wealthy.
- 4 will be financially secure.
- 5 will continue working, not because they want to but because they have to.
- 36 will be dead.
- 54 will be dead broke, dependent on their meager Social Security checks, relatives, friends, and even charity for a minimum standard living.

Only 5 percent of the 100 people are successful, and 95 percent are unsuccessful!

LIVING WEALTHY MINDSET

IT'S NO LONGER AN ISSUE OF DO YOU WANT TO BE A MILLIONAIRE; YOU HAVE TO BE A MILLIONAIRE TO LIVE A HALFWAY DECENT LIFE WHEN YOU ARE OLDER.

Do you want to be in the minority of the top 5 percent or do you want to join the majority in the 95 percent? I think I know your answer.

SEVEN STEPS FOR FINANCIAL TRACTION

When I set out to improve my financial situation, I first had to change my mindset. That's what the majority of this chapter has been about. Frankly, because it's the hardest part of the whole process. And it's a continual process; we never graduate from improving our mindset.

But at some point, we need to get traction.

LIVING WEALTHY MINDSET

A TRACK (PLAN), PLUS ACTION, EQUALS TRACTION!

If you want to get on the track to financial wealth, the following are the six action steps toward traction!

1. COMMIT

To commit may seem basic, even obvious. In fact, you may be tempted to skip right over this step, but I assure you, if you do, you'll remain stuck in a cycle of lack, no matter how much money you make.

Your commitment to multimillionaire status is so much stronger than a mere decision. With commitment, there is the resolve to do "Whatever It Takes" (WIT) to achieve Kingdom millionaire status. Your commitment, whether it's time, energy, or income, is vital to achieving your goals.

2. WEALTH IS KING BUT INCOME IS QUEEN

Nothing beats having an abundance of money coming in! You *must* seek a strong flow of income. Your income is the strongest wealth-building tool you have. This isn't just about starting a business. Actually, 75 percent of all millionaires work for someone else. Excelling in your profession is the initial goal. Then we can talk about multiple streams of income with side businesses and assets.

LIVING WEALTHY MINDSET

NOTHING CREATES FINANCIAL CONFIDENCE MORE THAN HAVING MULTIPLE CASH FLOWS.

---

3. INCREASE 10X YOUR INCOME TARGET

Most people miss their targets for the simple reason that they don't set their targets high enough in the first place. Here's what I mean. If you want to make $300,000 a year, you need to take action and operate like you are shooting for a $3,000,000 target. Those are very different strategies.

4. GET OUT OF BAD DEBT

Banks know you will be a millionaire plus over your lifetime, and they want to make sure they get the majority of the money you earn. You are

117

CONFIDENCE FOR LIVING WEALTHY

going to need a detailed strategic plan to eliminate all your consumer debt that you are paying 12-24 percent interest on. There are different plans you can use; there isn't a cookie cutter plan for everybody.

One of the first things you need to do is face your mountain of debt before you can faith it. That means sitting down with your spouse and figuring out the hard-core numbers about how much you actually owe. Then you both need to work together to destroy it. Remember, one puts 1,000 to flight, but two will put 10,000 to flight. Synergy accelerates the elimination of bad debt.

5. DO THE MATH

Doing the math is the best way to see the reality of what is required to get traction. Sometimes the numbers are so big they don't seem real. Targets can sometimes seem out of reach, almost overwhelming, which may lead to you giving up.

Math can reduce a big target down to some small daily adjustments in your actions which, over time, can make a big impact. So, try working backward from your target. Reverse engineer it. How much money, how many sales, how many customers, and how many promotions will it take to get there?

6. SAVE TO INVEST IN ASSETS

Pay yourself first before you pay your bills. This is the secret of the super wealthy. Most people spend all their money first, and then say they will save what is left over. Guess what happens? Every week, nothing is left over. Or most people only save for emergencies. And guess what they always have? One emergency after another.

You can save and become wealthy through the power of compound interest. It just takes a long time. The fast-track road to bad-debt elimination and wealth acceleration is to save money for capital to invest in an asset that produces a cash flow.

7. INVEST IN YOURSELF

Nobody can be great at anything without practicing and learning. You may not have a million dollars yet because you are missing

118

information. I can't do open heart surgery because I don't have the right information to pull it off. If I wanted to become a heart surgeon, I would need to invest in the knowledge required to perform the operation.

How can you expect to increase your income, become more valuable, or improve your ability to accumulate wealth from the economy without a significant investment of time and money?

These are the seven first steps in your Living Wealthy journey. Commit to growing your financial wealth intelligence, taking the correct, corresponding massive actions, to get you where you want to go.

Learn how to eliminate bad-debt and accelerate your financial wealth at www.KeithJohnson.tv/ConfidenceU

Have you made the decision to be *willing, worthy,* and *capable* of maximizing your potential in the area of wealth by becoming a millionaire? Yes!

ENDNOTE

1. Brian Tracy, *Goals! How to Get Everything You Want—Faster than You Ever Thought Possible* (San Francisco, CA: Berrett-Koehler Publishers, 2010), 6-7.

CHAPTER 11

THE SUPERNATURAL POWER OF 10

ALIGNING WEALTH FOR MORAL AND SPIRITUAL DISTRIBUTION

I was attending Ball State University in Muncie, Indiana, known at the time as the number one party school in the United States. I was a member of the Sigma Pi Epsilon fraternity, also known as the number one party fraternity. We played rugby every Saturday morning and one Saturday, after a Friday night of partying, I realized I had forgotten my cleats. I quickly jumped on my Honda 750 Nighthawk motorcycle and rushed down the back streets of Muncie going 65 miles an hour, in a 30 mile an hour zone.

A car pulled out in front of me from a side street. My bike slammed into the front fender of the car and I was launched about 50 feet in the air. While I was airborne, something amazing happened I'll never forget. I saw a big hand that looked like a huge Mickey Mouse glove come up under my butt and sit me down on the pavement.

I was completely knocked out, and when I woke up, I thought for sure I had major injuries. However, I could actually stand up and I walked away with no injuries. I knew God had supernaturally saved my life. And to be honest, this event scared the hell right out of me. Literally!

Something inside me said I needed to leave my home state of Indiana and move to Florida. I knew inside that if I didn't get away from my family and friends, I would never be able to change my life for the better.

MOVING ON

Leaving everything behind was really tough. I went from fun, wild parties every night to living in a different place knowing no one. I was 22 years of age, lonely, single, and living in a trailer park in a beat-up fifth wheel trailer that was all jacked up. The oven worked, but not the grill. The washing machine was broken, but the dryer worked, so I washed my clothes in the sink.

My motorcycle was destroyed in the wreck, so I bought an old $800 used car that had no air conditioning. When I went to my first job interview, it was 107 degrees. I was sweat-soaked by the time I arrived. Honestly, it felt like a dark cloud was surrounding me, and I lost all hope for the future. Fortunately, I landed the job at my first interview at a men's clothing store in the local mall.

LIVING WEALTHY MINDSET

GIVING BACK IS PROOF YOU HAVE CONQUERED A GREED AND POVERTY MENTALITY.

During that time, someone recommended a book to me. I don't remember the title, but the gist of it was—be a giver to the world rather than a taker by giving 10 percent of my income away. The book promised amazing changes that could happen in my life.

At that time I had nothing to lose. I was only making $100 per week. I remember going to the local Lutheran church across the street, and when the offering basket went by, I remember how hard it was to give my first 10 percent, that ten-dollar bill. Thoughts flooded my mind. *I could use that ten bucks to buy gas, bread, and peanut butter for lunches this week. Why does this church need my money? It looks like they're doing pretty good.* However, I knew I needed a change, so I took a risk and tried what the book said to do. I plopped my first $10 in the basket.

I was totally shocked how quickly things started to change. Two weeks later, a returning customer came into the clothing store and offered me a job that paid four times more than I was making. It even included a brand-new company car with air conditioning!

A month later, God brought a new and incredible Christian friend into my life. I have been married to her for 26 years. My broke, lonely, miserable days were over!

Today, I thank God I put my first $10 in the offering basket at church, for it has established one of the foundational principles for all the success in my life.

LIVING WEALTHY MINDSET

WHEN YOU ARE FAITHFUL IN THE SMALL AMOUNTS, GOD WILL MAKE YOU RESPONSIBLE OVER BIGGER AMOUNTS.

For way too long, the local church has been in financial ICU, on life support, due to a lack of financial resources. About 10,000 churches close their doors each year. Pastors are un-calling themselves by dropping out of ministry because they are grossly underpaid, under-appreciated, and burned out.

Most churches possess huge potential to make an impact on their region, but they are functioning in a crippled state because they lack funds needed to truly see transformation. Sadly, due to the lack of financial education, most of the congregation lack personal finances to support the local work in any significant way. So "one dollar" or "George Washington offerings" become the norm. This has to change!

The change must start in the heart of our dear precious pastors who must not allow the spirit of mammon to stop them from training, teaching, and educating themselves and their followers about money. It's time for pastors to realize their followers cannot rise any higher in their knowledge than their shepherd.

It's time for God's shepherds to take a stand and say, "I'm not going to put up with being broke anymore!" And it's time for congregations to want to see their pastors financially blessed by God, realizing that the anointing flows from the head down, according to Psalm 133:2. So if the pastor isn't financially blessed, the congregation won't be blessed.

That's why I want to inspire millions of new Kingdom millionaire philanthropists to give 10 percent of their income to the local church in order to economically jumpstart a fresh new movement.

When this happens, it will generate billions of dollars to be focused on expanding the Kingdom and to spreading the Gospel around the world. An excellent example of a millionaire who tithed 10 percent is the founder of Chick-fil-A.

CHICK-FIL-A FOUNDER SAMUEL TRUETT CATHY

The parking lot is packed; there is no place to park. The drive-through lane is full of cars, full of people waiting to buy a chicken sandwich that comes with a friendly smile and great service. What was the foundational strategy for the founder's success?

From the first days of marriage, he and his wife, Jeannette, had tithed 10 percent of their income. Cathy credits another inspiration for that practice as well: "Sir John Templeton, the [late] financial investment expert and creator of the Templeton Funds, tells audiences that the safest recommendation and the one that pays the highest dividend is tithing—giving 10 percent of your earnings to honor God in the way you see fit." Cathy once asked Templeton about it personally: "He confirmed the statement and added that he had never known anyone who had tithed for 10 years who was not rewarded."[2]

INSPIRING TESTIMONIES

History is filled with people who believed, accepted, and practiced Bible teachings on the Supernatural Power of 10. There is mention of patriarchs such as Abraham (Genesis 14:20), Jacob (Genesis 28:22), and even the whole nation of Israel. All of whom became very wealthy.

To my surprise, I discovered that many of America's early industrial fathers, who literally built America, also practiced the *Power of 10*.

There are stories of famous and wealthy people who credited the returning of the tithe to God as the secret for their success and prosperity. These individuals include: William Colgate of Colgate toothpaste, John D. Rockefeller Sr., Henry John Heinz of Heinz Ketchup, Milton S. Hershey of Hershey's Chocolate, and James Cash Penney of J.C. Penney.

Tithing is the best kept prosperity secret in existence. –Mark Victor Hanson, Coauthor, *Chicken Soup for the Soul* Series

The Kingdom millionaire knows that *giving* is the highest form of the manifestation of love that one can exhibit (John 3:16). It takes both *faith* and *action* to give back a portion when you have been blessed by God.

LIVING WEALTHY MINDSET

WEALTHY PEOPLE VIEW GIVING AS 100% X 10% = 1,000%. THIS IS SPIRITUAL SUPERNATURAL MATH.

Oprah has donated at least 10 percent of her annual income throughout her adult life. Even Kim Kardashian claims she has been giving 10 percent of her income from an early age. When looking behind the curtain of many financially wealthy people, the common denominator is—the more they gave, the more they received.

The act of giving multiplies your financial wealth 1,000-fold. Just like a seed multiplies when it's sown in the soil, money multiplies when it's given away.

People with a poverty mindset think that giving money away is throwing it away. They view giving as: 100% - 10% = 90%. This is logical math. If you try to figure it out mathematically, you will be stumped. But you believe, you will receive much more than 10 percent in return. It may show up as cash, or in new people, ideas, and opportunities that appear in your life supernaturally. You do the natural. Trust God to do the supernatural.

No matter where you are today financially, if you want to take your life to your full wealth potential of 10X as discussed in Chapter 2, it is essential to commit to giving 10 percent. God promised to multiply what you give.

Now may He who supplies seed to the sower, and bread for food, supply and **multiply** the seed you have sown and increase the fruits of your righteousness (2 Corinthians 9:10).

LIVING WEALTHY MINDSET

THE POWER OF 10 IS A MONEY MULTIPLIER, NOT A MONEY SUBTRACTOR.

This is the math Jesus talked about when He said your seed has the potential to produce 30, 60, and 100-fold return.

I was fortunate to spend time with one of the richest men in Australia, industrialist Peter J. Daniels. He said, "You cannot be greedy if you tithe."

I have noticed over the years that the Supernatural Power of 10 produces eight benefits to empower you to Living Wealthy:

1. Billion and million-dollar ideas
2. Financial increase
3. Job promotions
4. Divine connections
5. Open doors
6. Divine protection
7. Strategic plans
8. Solutions to problems

The Kingdom millionaire commits to giving 10 percent of all their income. Committing to this principle will make you richer than you ever dreamed possible.

JOHN D. ROCKEFELLER - THE FIRST BILLIONAIRE

The very first person to reach the status of billionaire was a man who knew how to set goals and follow through. Rockefeller, a devout Baptist and one of our nation's first billionaires, said, "I never would have been able to tithe the first million dollars I ever made if I had not tithed my first salary, which was $1.50 per week."

He believed that the ability to make money was a gift from God to be developed and used to the best of one's ability and for the good of humankind. At the age of 23, he had become a millionaire; and by the age of 50, a billionaire. Every decision, attitude, and relationship was tailored to create his personal power and wealth.

David Rockefeller said that when he was 7 years old he received an allowance of 50 cents a week. David was taught to save five cents and that the other five cents belonged to the Lord, his tithe to God. He said, "Our parents made us feel, from an early age, that we had to contribute, not just take."

J.L. KRAFT

J.L. Kraft was head of the Kraft Cheese Corporation, who gave approximately 25 percent of his enormous income to Christian causes for many years. He said, "The only investment I ever made which has paid consistently increasing dividends is the money I have given to the Lord."

ANTHONY T. ROSSI

Anthony Rossi came to the United States from Italy in the 1920s as a young teenager, with nothing but the clothes on his back. A Christian couple befriended him, and through their love, he came to know Christ as his Savior and Lord. One Sunday in church, he prayed, "Lord, if You give me an idea for a business, I will be faithful to give a portion of everything I make to Your work."

That very morning, the idea of "fresh-squeezed orange juice" popped into his head. He founded the Tropicana Company and was faithful to give God 50 percent of his income for 60 years!

HENRY P. CROWELL

Does the name Henry P. Crowell sound familiar to you? How about the company he founded, Quaker Oats? When a young man, Crowell heard a sermon by Dwight L. Moody and made a remarkable commitment to the Lord. He said, "I can't be a preacher, but I can be a good businessman." He prayed, "If you would let me make money, I will use it in Your service."

He bought a little run-down mill called Quaker Mill. Not only did he faithfully tithe, but it is reported that he gave far beyond the tithe and funded the Lord's work for more than 40 years.

WILLIAM COLGATE

Colgate read the Old Testament story of Jacob's vow. When Jacob left home, he said, "If God will be with me and will watch over me on this journey I am taking and will give me food to eat and clothes to wear so that I return safely to my father's house, then the Lord will be my God... and of all that You [God] give me I will give You a tenth" (Genesis 28:20-22).

Jacob's vow challenged Colgate. He made a similar vow; he determined to give God first place in his life, and he also promised to give a tenth, a tithe, of his profits to God.

Colgate never forgot his promise to God. From the first dollar he earned he devoted 10 percent of his net earnings to benevolence. As he prospered, he instructed his accountants to increase the amount to 20 percent and later to 30 percent. It seemed that the more he gave, the more he prospered.

William Colgate and Company met with success from the start. Within 6 years he added the manufacturing of starch to his laundry soap business. Later, he also produced hand soap and a variety of toilet and shaving soaps.

Colgate saw, in his business, the fulfillment of the promise made to tithe payers that God will "throw open the floodgates of heaven and pour out so much blessing that you will not have room enough for it" (Malachi 3:10).

The two founders of Holiday Inn, Wallace Johnson and Kemmons Wilson; Thomas Welch of Welch's Grape Juice; and David Green, founder of Hobby Lobby are also examples of godly men who committed themselves to the Power of 10. In doing so, they reaped billions of dollars and have had impact and influence in our society for generations.

THE MIRACLE RAIN IN PORT ELIZABETH, SOUTH AFRICA

Prior to my arriving to teach my first Confidence for Living Wealthy conference, Port Elizabeth had been suffering from the worst drought in more than 20 years. I spoke on the Supernatural Power of 10 in three Sunday services, challenging the congregation to commit to giving 10 percent of their income to their local church. The results were shocking! More than 700 forms were filled out by people making a commitment.

During the end of the last service, while I was speaking, suddenly I saw a cloud forming in the sky. And I heard the Holy Spirit say, "It's going to rain." I told the congregation the rain is coming because of the decisions they made that day. When we make a commitment, providence starts moving.

Early the next morning as I stepped out of my hotel, buckets of rain were falling. That same day I started to receive reports from people how miraculous things were happening in different people's lives in that congregation.

No surprise to me.

LIVING WEALTHY MINDSET
GOD CONFIRMS HIS PRINCIPLES WITH AMAZING MIRACLES.

For more than 26 years, I have put this principle to the test, and it has worked for me. I have been a very blessed man. Only with the help of God could a young boy who could hardly read and write experience the joy and abundance I have. It will work for you if you have the confidence to stop clenching what's in your hand. Remember, all good things come from God, so what you have in your hand, He placed there.

You can begin maximizing your wealth potential right away. Right now, set aside 10 percent. Put the cash aside, write a check to your church, give online, whatever the case may be, commit to the Supernatural Power of 10 today. You will be blessed.

ENDNOTE

1. John J. Miller, "Service with a Smile," *Philanthropy Roundtable,* Fall 2008; http://www.philanthropyroundtable.org/topic/excellence_in_philanthropy/service_with_a_smile; accessed November 18, 2017.

"WE DEVELOP WORLD-CLASS LEADERS WHO WILL MAKE A POSITIVE CHANGE IN THE WORLD."

I have dedicated my life to investing in the next generation of leaders through Destiny College International. We want to establish 100 new Christian colleges in the next 10 years.

Will you join forces with me in using your wealth to empower those who want to learn and grow but don't have the resources for classes, books, and supplies?

Consider being the answer to a world crying out for a new breed of leaders who have the godly leadership traits of Confidence, Competence, and Character.

Consider supporting one of our students living in developing countries who yearns for a quality college education.

For only $87 a month, you can supply 5 students with training. For $1,000 a month, you can help us establish a Christian leadership college for an entire year.

Thank you,
Keith Johnson, PhD

TO DONATE:
DestinyCollegeOnline.com/Donate

MAIL:
Destiny College International
PO Box 15001
Spring Hill, FL 34604
Call: 352-597-8775

Destiny College International is designed to put you on an accelerated fast-track to personal growth and transformation. DCI is unique because we focus on growing your leadership skills from a biblical worldview.

WHY ENROLL?

- World-Class Instructors
- Learn at Your Own Pace
- Low Financial Investment
- Accelerated Learning Program
- Partial Scholarships Now Available
- Credit for Ministry Life Experience
- Online Access

WOLRD CLASS INSTRUCTORS:

- Dr. John Maxwell, Rated #1 Leadership Strategist in the World
- Dr. Sam Chand, Internationally Known Leadership Expert
- Dr. John P. Kelly, President of International Coalition of Apostolic Leaders
- Dr. Vivian Rodgers, Known as Mr. Excellence in South Africa
- Dr. Bob Harrison, Dr. Increase and known as America's #1 Increase Authority.
- Bobb Biehl, Consultant to the top Christian Leaders in the Evangelical Movement
- Flip Flippen, Leader of one of the fastest-growing corporate and personal training companies.
- Dr. Robb Thompson, Relationship Expert
- Dr. Keith Johnson, America's #1 Confidence Coach, Leadership Expert
- Dr. Dave Williams, America's Pacesetting Leadership Coach, and many more.
- Dr. Myles Munroe, Teaching from the late, great and renowned expert on Leadership Strategies.

LEARN MORE AND APPLY TODAY:
www.DestinyCollegeOnline.com

LIVING WEALTHY — EXPERIENCE

Feeling the pressure of a lack in financial support for your ministry?

In 2017, more than 4,000 churches closed their doors because they couldn't get the finances needed to sustain the ministry. Leaders, many just like you, gave up on their God-given dreams because they didn't have the resources to make those dreams a reality.

Dow Jones may be at an all-time high, but church giving is at an all-time low.

The numbers just don't add up. Why are church finances declining if the economy is expanding? While many ministry leaders are experts in the realm of spirituality, they lack practical wisdom and knowledge of financial issues. When many of us compare our destiny with our current bank account, we reduce the size of the dream to the size of our wallet.

Introducing the Living Wealthy Experience

The Living Wealthy Experience does two things to help solve the problem of financial lack:

1. On Sunday morning, I will speak an inspirational message on the Power of Ten to grow the number of people committed to tithing to your church.

2. On Sunday night, my wife, Bonnie, and I will share proven principles on how we got out of $180,000 of bad debt and accelerated our path to wealth. This personal experience alone will give your congregation a clear strategy on how to multiply their income and increase their giving to fulfill their God-given destiny.

LEARN MORE ABOUT HOW YOU CAN HOST A
LIVING WEALTHY EXPERIENCE AT:
www.KeithJohnson.tv/LWE

CONFIDENCE UNIVERSITY

This platform is a world-class training system that introduces the three pillars of success and significance:

- CONFIDENCE
- LEADERSHIP
- WEALTH

In ConfidenceU, you will learn the necessary mindset and skillset to maximize your full potential in every area of life.

Whether you're leading a church, launching a business, or building a better you, this training system is designed to take you to a whole new level.

LEARN MORE ABOUT CONFIDENCE U BY VISITING:
www.KeithJohnson.tv/ConfidenceU

ABOUT THE AUTHOR

D R. KEITH JOHNSON, AMERICA'S #1 CONFIDENCE COACH, has spent the past 20 years helping leaders of businesses, organizations, ministries, and churches become successful with his keynote messages, coaching programs, and training tools. Dr. Johnson has spoken in person to thousands of people worldwide including Japan, Singapore, Malaysia, Indonesia, Africa, India, Spain, Bahamas, Canada, Scotland, France, Mexico, Costa Rica and throughout the United States. His website (www.keithjohnson.tv) reaches countless people seeking to improve their lives in a myriad of ways. He is the founder and CEO of Keith Johnson International and the chancellor of Destiny International College. He and his wife, Bonnie, live in the Tampa Bay area of Florida.

CONTACT INFORMATION

Keith Johnson International

PO Box 15001

Spring Hill, FL 34604

Telephone: 352-597-8775

Booking@keithjohnson.tv

LET'S CONNECT

@DrKeithJohnson

67499282R00076

Made in the USA
Columbia, SC
01 August 2019